The
Blueprint

Also from Eatms Productions

Evil and the Mountain Ungreed
Project 2025 The List
Stoic Principles Reimagined for Modern Challenges
Project 2025, Christian Dumb Dumbs, & The Republican Agenda
Self Help for American Billionaires A Parody
4B- BURN, BAN, BOYCOTT, BUILD
Selfish Steve Empathy Island
Tariffs, Taxes, & Face Eating Leopards
How to Survive in Post America as a Woman Project 2025

Project 2025: The Blueprint

By
Esme Mees

An
Eatms Production

ISBN: 978-1-966014-02-7

Cover, interior design, interior prints by: Esme Mees

eatms@pm.me
Printed in the United States of America.

4

Comfort is the enemy of progress.

-P.T. Barnum

Introduction

Project 2025: Presidential Transition Project isn't just another political maneuver—it's a theocratic, Christo-fascist blueprint that threatens to dismantle American democracy and reverberate across the globe. This is not a drill; it's a calculated assault on our freedoms, our diversity, and our very way of life. Imagine a government ruled by a radical religious ideology. Project 2025 aims to infuse every aspect of governance with extreme right wing "Christian" values, sidelining the separation of church and state. This means laws and policies will be dictated by a narrow, exclusionary interpretation of Christianity, marginalizing anyone who doesn't fit this mold and threatening to return society to the dark ages.

The plan seeks to centralize power in the executive branch, undermining the checks and balances that safeguard our democracy. This consolidation of power paves the way for authoritarian rule, where dissent is crushed, and the will of the few overrides the rights of the many. Socially, the implications are dire. Women's reproductive rights will be obliterated, LGBTQ+ protections will be gutted, and religious exemptions will allow rampant discrimination. This isn't about preserving freedom—it's about enforcing a rigid, oppressive social order that strips away hard-won rights and liberties.

The impact won't stop at our borders. Project 2025's environmental deregulation and aggressive foreign policy will have global repercussions. Expect increased pollution, accelerated climate change, and heightened international tensions. The world will feel the shockwaves of America's retreat into isolationist, destructive policies. This is more than a policy shift—it's a terrifying transformation with catastrophic consequences. Project 2025 is a Christo-fascist endgame, aiming to reshape America into a theocratic, authoritarian state with disastrous effects worldwide. Stay vigilant, stay informed, and be ready to fight for the democratic, inclusive world we all deserve. The stakes couldn't be higher.

Esme Mees, Summer 2024

Table of Contents

The Blueprint

Project 2025 is a collection of far right "Christian" nationalist policy proposals designed to overhaul the U.S. government if a Republican wins the presidency in 2024. Created by the Heritage Foundation, this monstrous plan, 920 pages, aims to push a radical "Christian" nationalist agenda, stripping rights and protections. It is a nightmare scenario for democracy, civil liberties, international relations, and the environment.

Here is their plan-

Mandate for Leadership
The Conservative Promise
Project 2025: Presidential Transition Project

Section 3: The General Welfare

Section 4: The Economy

Section 5: Independent Regulatory Agencies

ONWARD! By Edwin Feulner

Forward: A Promise to America
by Kevin Roberts

- A Cautionary Tale

Gather round, everyone, for the story you are about to hear is more terrifying than you can imagine. "Project 2025: Introduction - A Promise to America" by Kevin Roberts isn't just an innocuous title. It's a terrifying outline for turning America into a theocratic, Christo-fascist state. What we're looking at here is not a simple political shift but a radical transformation with consequences that will dismantle democracy and impose an oppressive order domestically and globally.

The Theocratic Takeover

Let's start with the most chilling aspect of all: the theocratic takeover. Roberts and his allies envision a government that's deeply infused with conservative Christian values. This isn't about protecting religious freedom—it's about imposing a narrow, exclusionary interpretation of Christianity on everyone. Imagine a government where policies are dictated not by the Constitution but by a particular religious dogma. The separation of church and state? Gone. In its place, a system where religious doctrine trumps individual rights and freedoms. If you don't fit into their narrow view of morality, you'll find yourself marginalized and oppressed.

Authoritarian Power Grab

Project 2025 seeks to centralize power within the executive branch, undermining the checks and balances that are fundamental to our democracy. Roberts' vision involves appointing loyalists to key positions, ensuring that every branch of government, from the judiciary to federal agencies, aligns with their agenda. This consolidation of power means that dissenting voices will be silenced, and democratic processes will be bypassed. It's authoritarian rule where the whims of a few override the rights and freedoms of the many. Imagine a country where critical decisions impacting millions are made unilaterally, without debate, oversight, or opposition.

Economic and Social Regression

Economically and socially, Project 2025 promises a return to a darker era. Roberts champions deregulation, tax cuts for the wealthy, and privatization of public services. This might sound like economic freedom, but in reality, it means increased inequality, reduced public services, and a society where the rich get richer while the rest struggle to make ends meet. The elimination of overtime pay is also on the chopping block. Deregulation will gut environmental protections, consumer safeguards, and worker rights, creating a free-for-all where corporate profits are prioritized over public well-being. Privatization will transform essential services like healthcare and education into commodities, making them inaccessible to those who can't afford the exorbitant costs.

Socially Regressive Policies

Socially, the implications are equally dire. Women's reproductive rights will be obliterated. Expect severe restrictions on access to abortion and contraception, all under the guise of protecting life and religious freedom. LGBTQ+ protections will be gutted, and discrimination will be allowed to flourish unchecked. Religious exemptions will enable businesses and service providers to deny services based on their beliefs, effectively sanctioning bigotry and exclusion. This isn't about preserving freedom; it's about enforcing a rigid, oppressive social order that strips away hard-won rights and liberties. Imagine living in a society where your rights depend on your ability to conform to a narrow, exclusionary definition of morality.

Environmental Catastrophe

Environmental policies under Project 2025 will be a disaster. Roberts' vision includes aggressive deregulation and prioritization of fossil fuel interests. This means more drilling, mining, and deforestation, leading to increased pollution and accelerated climate change. Public lands will be handed over to private interests for exploitation, endangering our natural heritage and public health. The consequences will be felt globally, as the U.S. retreats from international environmental agreements and undermines efforts to combat climate change.

Imagine a world where environmental degradation accelerates unchecked, leading to more extreme weather, loss of biodiversity, and greater health risks.

Global Consequences

The impact of Project 2025 won't stop at our borders. Roberts' vision for an aggressive foreign policy and militarization will have global repercussions. Expect increased defense spending at the expense of social programs, and a more assertive stance on the global stage that risks escalating conflicts. This military-first approach prioritizes armed strength over diplomatic solutions, heightening international tensions and reducing global stability. Imagine a world where the U.S. is seen not as a leader in peace and democracy but as an aggressor, prioritizing power and domination over cooperation and justice.

Suppressing Dissent

Roberts is well aware that these sweeping changes will not be universally welcomed. Project 2025 includes strategies to control public perception and suppress dissent. This means dominating the media narrative, leveraging conservative media outlets, and using social media to spread their message while discrediting and marginalizing opposing viewpoints. Legal and administrative measures will be employed to stifle protests and opposition, including stricter laws on public assembly, increased surveillance, and harsher penalties for dissent. Imagine living in a society where speaking out against the government can lead to severe repercussions, where the freedom to protest and express dissent is curtailed.

Conclusion

"Project 2025: Introduction - A Promise to America" by Kevin Roberts lays out a Christo-fascist takeover of America. This plan aims to dismantle democracy, centralize power, and impose a rigid, oppressive social order. The consequences will be felt not only within the U.S. but globally, as environmental degradation accelerates, international tensions rise, and democratic values are undermined.

Why We Can't Trust Kevin Roberts

We can't trust Kevin Roberts because his background and actions reveal a dangerous agenda. As president of the Heritage Foundation, he has a history of pushing extreme conservative policies that threaten our democracy. Roberts has used his platform to influence the appointment of conservative judges, like Justices Neil Gorsuch, Brett Kavanaugh, and Amy Coney Barrett, to the Supreme Court. This conservative stronghold can dismantle civil liberties and roll back rights that took decades to secure, all under the guise of strict constitutionalism. Roberts is also a hypocrite because, while he champions conservative values and austerity for the general public, the Foundation receives millions in dark money contributions to push its agenda. His stance on smaller government contradicts his using executive power to enforce unpopular far right overreach of power.

Roberts' economic stance is equally terrifying. Before leading the Heritage Foundation, he was the executive vice president of the Texas Public Policy Foundation, where he honed his skills in advocating for deregulation and tax cuts for the wealthy. His support for the 2017 Tax Cuts and Jobs Act is a prime example. This act benefited the richest Americans and corporations while ballooning the national deficit. Roberts also backs aggressive deregulation, reminiscent of the Trump administration's rollback of over 100 environmental regulations, which increased pollution and put public health at risk. His policies prioritize corporate profits over the welfare of everyday Americans, exacerbating economic inequality.

Socially, Roberts' background is a blueprint for regression. At the Texas Public Policy Foundation, he championed efforts to limit reproductive rights and healthcare access, a stance he carried into his tenure at the Heritage Foundation. He supports policies that severely restrict access to abortion and contraception, jeopardizing women's health and autonomy. Roberts also advocates for religious exemptions that allow businesses to discriminate against LGBTQ+ individuals. His actions reveal a clear intent to impose a narrow, exclusionary vision of society, undermining the rights and freedoms of those who don't conform. We can't trust Kevin Roberts because his history and actions, especially pertaining to deregulating the government, threaten to transform America into an authoritarian, theocratic state with dire consequences for our democracy and individual liberties.

Note on Impoundment

The use of impoundment to dismantle government agencies is a frightening strategy rooted in historical abuses of executive power. Impoundment occurs when the President refuses to spend money that Congress has appropriated, effectively nullifying the legislative branch's budgetary decisions. This tactic was famously employed by President Richard Nixon in the early 1970s, leading to significant political and legal battles. Nixon's extensive use of impoundment to defund programs he opposed prompted Congress to pass the Congressional Budget and Impoundment Control Act of 1974, which aimed to curb such executive overreach by requiring the President to obtain congressional approval for rescissions of appropriated funds.

Roberts, conservative think tanks, and Russ Vought, a prominent figure in Project 2025 and a likely candidate for Chief of Staff under a potential second Trump administration, advocate for the revival and expansion of impoundment as a means to dismantle government agencies. Vought's plan involves using this tactic to cripple agencies like the Environmental Protection Agency (EPA) and the Department of Education, effectively neutralizing their ability to enforce regulations and provide essential services. This strategy aims to dismantle the administrative state, a goal that aligns with their broader agenda to reduce government intervention and oversight.

This strategy is part of a broader agenda to weaken government oversight and regulation. The implications of this strategy are terrifying, particularly when considered in the context of the unitary executive theory. This theory posits that all executive power is vested in the president, granting him or her broad control over the entire executive branch. Impoundment, would effectively extend this theory, allowing the president to bypass Congress and unilaterally decide which programs and agencies receive funding. Using impoundment to defund key agencies could lead to a significant rollback of protections for public health, the environment, and consumer rights. It represents a dangerous encroachment on the separation of powers, allowing the executive branch to override the will of Congress and undermine the checks and balances that are fundamental to democratic governance. Reviving such tactics is a severe reminder of how fragile our institutions can be when subjected to the whims of those who prioritize ideological agendas over the common good.

Section 1:
Taking the Reins of Government
1 White House Office
by Rick Dearborn

- A Cautionary Tale

Attention please! What is about to be revealed will leave you speechless and utterly horrified. Rick Dearborn's "Taking the Reins of Government: White House Office" is the first section of Project 2025, and it's an unsettling manual on seizing and wielding power within the highest office of the United States for a radical, authoritarian transformation of our government.

This document is an unnerving guide for transforming the White House into a bastion of conservative power. This document meticulously details a plan to centralize authority, streamline operations, and ensure unwavering adherence to a conservative agenda. Dearborn's vision is one of precision and control, aiming to reshape the very essence of American governance.

Dearborn begins by emphasizing the necessity of staffing the White House with loyalists. He stresses the importance of selecting individuals who are not only skilled but ideologically aligned with conservative principles. This focus on loyalty over merit raises alarms about the potential erosion of expertise and the creation of an echo chamber where dissent is stifled, and critical perspectives are marginalized.

The document outlines strategies for reducing bureaucratic red tape, advocating for a streamlined White House operation. While efficiency is often a worthy goal, Dearborn's approach appears designed to facilitate rapid policy implementation without the checks and balances necessary for fair governance. The streamlined processes he proposes prioritize speed over deliberation, risking the bypassing of thorough analysis and debate.

A major component of the manual addresses the relationship between the White House and federal agencies. Dearborn recommends placing trusted allies in key agency positions and using executive

19

orders to direct their activities. These measures threaten the independence of federal agencies, which are intended to function autonomously to serve the public impartially, free from political influence.

Dearborn also suggests strategies for influencing the judiciary by ensuring the appointment of judges who will support the administration's policies. This involves close collaboration with the Senate to expedite confirmations. Such influence over the judiciary risks undermining its independence and compromising the checks and balances crucial to a democratic system.

In the realm of communications, Dearborn highlights the importance of controlling the narrative and managing the media. He advises employing strategic messaging to shape public perception and using a robust communications team to handle crises and promote the administration's achievements. This focus on media manipulation raises concerns about the marginalization of dissenting voices and the potential for propaganda.

The manual advocates for aggressive policy initiatives, particularly in deregulation, tax reform, and national security. Dearborn outlines an agenda aimed at rolling back regulations that protect the environment and public health, reducing taxes mainly for the wealthy, and adopting a more confrontational foreign policy. These policies reflect a commitment to free-market principles and strong national defense, often at the expense of social welfare and international cooperation.

In summary, "Taking the Reins of Government" by Rick Dearborn is a comprehensive playbook for consolidating power within the White House and steering the government in a sharply conservative direction. Its detailed strategies for staffing, streamlining, and controlling various branches of government reveal a determined effort to reshape American governance. Dearborn's vision, marked by precision and ambition, serves as an urgent reminder of the fragility of democratic institutions and the ever-present risk of authoritarianism. The document's chilling precision and calculated strategies should prompt serious reflection on the future of democracy and the protection of its core principles.

Why We Can't Trust Rick Dearborn

We can't trust Rick Dearborn due to his background and actions, which reveal a dangerous agenda. As Deputy Chief of Staff under President Trump, Dearborn played a pivotal role in implementing extreme conservative policies that centralized power within the executive branch. His influence extended to filling key government positions with loyalists, ensuring that every decision aligned with their agenda. This strategy undermined the essential checks and balances of our democracy, paving the way for authoritarian control where dissent is not tolerated.

Dearborn's economic policies are equally alarming. During his time in the Trump administration, he supported massive tax cuts for the wealthy, embodied in the 2017 Tax Cuts and Jobs Act. This legislation disproportionately benefited the richest Americans while adding trillions to the national deficit. Moreover, Dearborn was a staunch advocate for deregulation, pushing to roll back over 100 environmental regulations, which led to increased pollution and health risks. His tenure also saw efforts to privatize public services like healthcare and education, making essential services inaccessible to those who need them most and widening the gap between the rich and the poor.

Socially, Dearborn's vision is deeply regressive. He supported policies that restricted reproductive rights, as seen in the administration's attempts to defund Planned Parenthood and limit access to contraception and abortion services. His influence extended to rolling back protections for LGBTQ+ individuals, promoting religious exemptions that allowed discrimination. This approach wasn't about preserving freedom; it was about enforcing a narrow, exclusionary interpretation of Christian values. Additionally, Dearborn's tactics to suppress dissent included controlling the narrative through conservative media and employing legal measures to stifle opposition, creating a climate of fear and suppressing democratic debate. We can't trust Rick Dearborn because his background and actions aim to transform America into an authoritarian state with disastrous consequences for democracy and individual freedoms.

Section 1:
Taking the Reins of Government
2 Executive Office of the President of the United States
by Russ Vought

- A Cautionary Tale

The bad dream continues and is very real. "Taking the Reins of Power: Executive Office of the President of the United States" by Russ Vought is a chilling blueprint for a radical transformation of the American government. The document is a step-by-step guide to consolidating power within the executive branch, reducing the influence of federal agencies, and enforcing a stringent conservative agenda. It paints a picture of a government streamlined for efficiency, but at the cost of democratic principles and checks and balances. Vought's vision is one of centralized control and unwavering ideological purity, where loyalty to the cause is paramount.

The plan emphasizes the appointment of ideologically aligned loyalists who are committed to the conservative cause. Vought stresses the importance of reducing the size and influence of federal agencies, suggesting that many of them be either downsized or eliminated entirely. This includes significant cuts to social programs and a rollback of regulatory measures that protect the environment and public health. The guide advocates for an aggressive stance on national security, prioritizing military spending over social welfare initiatives.

A particularly alarming aspect of Vought's roadmap is its focus on undermining the independence of the judiciary. The document outlines strategies for appointing judges who will adhere to conservative principles, thereby ensuring that court decisions align with their ideological goals. This threatens the impartiality of the judicial system and poses a serious risk to the principle of checks and balances that is fundamental to American democracy.

Vought's plan also calls for a significant reduction in the influence of independent agencies. It suggests that these agencies be brought under tighter control of the executive branch, effectively eroding their ability to operate independently. This would lead to a government where dissenting voices are minimized, if not entirely silenced, and where the executive branch holds near-absolute authority. The tone of the document is unapologetically ambitious, leaving little room for opposition or deviation from its prescribed path.

Environmental protections are a major target in this blueprint. Vought advocates for dismantling many of the regulations that safeguard natural resources and public health. The emphasis is on economic growth and deregulation, often at the expense of long-term sustainability and environmental stewardship. This approach could have devastating consequences for the planet, prioritizing short-term gains over the well-being of future generations.

The roadmap also envisions significant changes to social welfare programs. Vought calls for cuts to funding for public health initiatives and social safety nets, arguing that these programs create dependency and stifle individual initiative. This perspective ignores the vital role these programs play in supporting vulnerable populations and ensuring a basic standard of living for all Americans. The proposed cuts would disproportionately impact the poor, elderly, and disabled, exacerbating existing inequalities.

National security is another area where Vought advocates for an aggressive approach. The document prioritizes military spending and a robust defense posture, often at the expense of diplomatic efforts and international cooperation. This hawkish stance risks escalating tensions with other nations and undermining global stability. The focus on military strength over diplomatic engagement reflects a broader trend in Vought's vision of governance: a preference for force and control over collaboration and consensus-building.

In essence, "Taking the Reins of Power" is a manifesto for a radical shift towards authoritarian governance under the guise of restoring constitutional principles. It's an urgent reminder of how fragile democratic institutions can be and how easily they can be reshaped by those with the will and the means to do so. The chilling precision and calculated strategies outlined in this document serve as a wake-up call to the potential dangers of concentrated power and the erosion of democratic norms.

Why We Can't Trust Russ Vought

We cannot trust Russ Vought because his background and actions reveal a consistent pattern of extreme partisanship and ideological rigidity. Vought, a key architect behind the Trump administration's budget policies, is known for his aggressive stance on slashing social programs and pushing for conservative priorities. His tenure as Director of the Office of Management and Budget (OMB) was marked by proposals to significantly cut funding for critical social services, including Medicaid, food assistance, and housing programs, which disproportionately affect the most vulnerable in society.

Moreover, Vought's deep connections to conservative think tanks, particularly the Heritage Foundation, further raise concerns about his commitment to an unbiased and balanced approach to governance. The Heritage Foundation, known for its hardline conservative agenda, has been instrumental in shaping policies that prioritize deregulation, tax cuts for the wealthy, and reductions in social welfare programs. Vought's alignment with these principles suggests a governance style that favors the wealthy and powerful at the expense of ordinary citizens.

Vought's personal advocacy for using impoundment to undermine government agencies highlights his willingness to bypass legislative authority and disrupt the balance of power. This tactic, reminiscent of President Nixon's notorious use of impoundment, underscores Vought's readiness to engage in executive overreach to achieve his conservative goals. His alignment with the unitary executive theory further amplifies concerns about his trustworthiness. This theory posits that all executive power is concentrated in the president, granting broad control over the executive branch. Vought's endorsement of this theory suggests a dangerous expansion of presidential power, undermining democratic checks and balances and increasing the risk of authoritarian governance.

Russ Vought's history of partisanship, his ties to influential conservative organizations, and his support for policies that centralize power and dismantle social safety nets make him a figure whose intentions and actions warrant deep skepticism and distrust. His vision of governance poses a significant threat to democratic principles and the equitable treatment of all citizens.

Section 1:
Taking the Reins of Government
3 Central Personnel Agencies: Managing the Bureaucracy
by Donald Devine, Dennis Dean Kirk, and Paul Dans

- A Cautionary Tale

Everyone, hold on, because this is going to be deeply unsettling. It's a foreboding sign that a tale of managing bureaucracy takes more people to write than any other section. "Taking the Reins of Government: Central Personnel Agencies: Managing the Bureaucracy" by Donald Devine, Dennis Dean Kirk, and Paul Dans is a daunting manual for overhauling the federal workforce and reshaping the administrative state.

This document is a meticulous guide on transforming the bureaucratic machinery to align it strictly with conservative values. The authors propose a comprehensive strategy to manage and control the vast network of government personnel, aiming to create a more compliant and ideologically uniform bureaucracy.

Devine, Kirk, and Dans begin by emphasizing the need for a dramatic shift in the culture of federal agencies. They argue that the current bureaucratic structure is plagued by inefficiency and ideological biases that hinder effective governance. Their solution is to instill a new culture rooted in conservative principles, prioritizing loyalty and alignment with the administration's agenda over traditional civil service values like neutrality and competence. The rush to cut red tape overlooks the fact that many regulations exist to prevent abuse, ensure fairness, and protect the public.

The manual details methods for appointing key personnel who share the administration's vision. The authors stress the importance of filling senior positions with individuals who are committed to the conservative cause and capable of driving the desired changes. This approach risks sidelining experienced and non-partisan professionals, potentially leading to a loss of expertise and institutional memory critical for effective governance.

The authors begin by arguing that the federal bureaucracy is bloated and inefficient, a claim often made by conservative thinkers. They suggest that significant cuts to the federal workforce are necessary to streamline operations and reduce government spending. However, this perspective dangerously overlooks the critical functions that many federal employees perform, from ensuring public safety to providing essential social services. Reducing the workforce so drastically could lead to a deterioration in the quality of services that Americans rely on, disproportionately affecting the most vulnerable populations.

One of the most alarming aspects of their proposal is the emphasis on implementing Schedule F, a controversial executive order introduced during the Trump administration. Schedule F would reclassify a large number of federal employees as at-will workers, stripping them of civil service protections and making it easier to hire and fire them based on political considerations. This move threatens to politicize the federal workforce, undermining the principle of a non-partisan civil service that operates based on merit rather than political loyalty. The potential for political purges and the erosion of professional standards in federal agencies is a dire threat to the stability and integrity of government operations.

Furthermore, the authors advocate for reducing the power and influence of federal unions, which they argue protect underperforming employees and obstruct necessary reforms. However, weakening unions would strip workers of essential protections and bargaining power, potentially leading to lower wages, worse working conditions, and a less motivated workforce. Federal employees, including those in critical roles such as healthcare, education, and public safety, could see their job security and working conditions deteriorate, impacting the quality of services they provide.

In summary, "Taking the Reins of Government: Central Personnel Agencies: Managing the Bureaucracy" by Devine, Kirk, and Dans is a thorough playbook for transforming the federal workforce to align with a loyalist agenda. A more ideologically uniform bureaucracy, driven by loyalty and stringent performance metrics, poses risks to the principles of non-partisan public service and effective governance. The precision and ambition of their strategies highlight the fragility of democratic institutions and the potential dangers of politicizing the civil service. This document serves as a timely reminder of the need to safeguard the integrity and independence of the federal workforce to ensure it can serve the public interest impartially and effectively.

Why We Can't Trust Donald Devine

We cannot trust Donald Devine because his background and actions reveal a consistent pattern of prioritizing radical downsizing and deregulation over the essential functions of government and the welfare of its citizens. As the former director of the U.S. Office of Personnel Management (OPM) under President Ronald Reagan, Devine was a key architect of significant cuts to federal staffing and the decentralization of authority. While he touted these changes as efforts to reduce bureaucratic inefficiencies, they often disregarded the critical services that federal employees provide, risking a hollowing out of government capabilities.

One notable example of Devine's controversial approach is his aggressive push for reducing the size of the federal workforce. During his tenure at the OPM, Devine implemented policies aimed at cutting federal jobs and transferring responsibilities to state and local governments. This strategy, while aimed at reducing federal spending, often led to a reduction in the quality and availability of essential services. For instance, cutting staffing levels in regulatory agencies can lead to insufficient oversight, which in turn can result in increased corporate malfeasance, environmental degradation, and public health risks. Devine's focus on downsizing prioritizes cost-cutting over maintaining robust and effective government operations.

Moreover, Devine's long-standing advocacy for deregulation poses significant risks to public welfare. He has consistently argued that deregulating various sectors of the economy will spur innovation and growth. However, this perspective fails to recognize the protective role that regulations play in safeguarding consumers, workers, and the environment. Deregulation can lead to reduced safety standards, increased pollution, and the exploitation of workers, undermining the public's trust in government institutions. Devine's ideological commitment to minimizing government oversight, regardless of the consequences, makes his policies deeply dire and untrustworthy. His background and actions suggest a disregard for the complexities of governance and a willingness to sacrifice public well-being for ideological purity.

Why We Can't Trust Dennis Dean Kirk

We cannot trust Dennis Dean Kirk because his background and actions reveal a consistent pattern of undermining worker protections and weakening the federal workforce's capacity to advocate for fair treatment and resources. As the former chairman of the Federal Labor Relations Authority (FLRA), Kirk has a history of promoting policies that limit the power of federal unions and reduce protections for federal employees. While he claims these measures are intended to increase efficiency and accountability, they often result in eroding the rights and morale of the workforce, ultimately harming the quality of public services.

One notable example of Kirk's controversial approach is his push to curtail collective bargaining rights. During his tenure, Kirk implemented policies that made it more difficult for federal unions to negotiate on behalf of their members. By restricting the scope of bargaining and limiting union access to resources, Kirk weakened the unions' ability to effectively represent federal employees. This not only undermines the unions' role in securing fair wages, benefits, and working conditions but also diminishes workers' ability to voice concerns and advocate for improvements. Such actions create a more hostile and less supportive work environment, which can lead to decreased employee satisfaction and productivity.

Moreover, Kirk's stance on reducing protections for federal employees further underscores his problematic approach. He has consistently advocated for policies that make it easier to discipline and terminate federal workers, arguing that this increases accountability and performance. However, this perspective overlooks the importance of due process and job security in maintaining a motivated and competent workforce. By stripping away protections, Kirk's policies expose employees to arbitrary and potentially politically motivated actions, which can deter talented individuals from pursuing or remaining in public service. His actions suggest a preference for weakening the structures that support a fair and effective federal workforce, making his policies deeply worrisome and untrustworthy. Kirk's background indicates a disregard for the well-being and rights of federal employees, posing significant risks to the integrity and effectiveness of public service.

Why We Can't Trust Paul Dans

We cannot trust Paul Dans because his background and actions reveal a consistent pattern of prioritizing political loyalty over competence and undermining the impartiality of the federal workforce. As a former chief of staff at the Office of Personnel Management (OPM) and a key figure in the Trump administration's efforts to reform the federal workforce, Dans has been a vocal advocate for policies that make it easier to hire and fire federal employees based on political considerations. This approach threatens the fundamental principles of a merit-based civil service and risks turning federal agencies into politically driven entities.

One notable example of Dans's controversial approach is his support for the "Schedule F" executive order, which aimed to reclassify thousands of federal employees into a new category that would strip them of civil service protections. By reclassifying these employees, Dans sought to make it easier to terminate them without the usual due process protections. This move, justified as a way to increase accountability, instead jeopardizes the independence of the civil service by making it more susceptible to political pressure. Such a policy could lead to the dismissal of career professionals who prioritize objective and nonpartisan execution of their duties, replacing them with individuals whose primary qualification is political loyalty.

Moreover, Dans's broader stance on federal workforce reforms highlights his problematic approach. He has consistently pushed for measures that reduce job security and weaken protections for federal employees, arguing that these steps are necessary to enhance performance and accountability. However, this perspective fails to recognize the importance of a stable and secure workforce in maintaining effective government operations. By undermining job security and due process protections, Dans's policies risk creating an environment where federal employees are more concerned with political survival than with carrying out their duties impartially and effectively. His actions suggest a preference for politicizing the civil service, making his policies deeply unnerving and untrustworthy. Dans's background and approach indicate a willingness to sacrifice the principles of fair and impartial public service for political expediency, posing significant risks to the integrity and functionality of the federal government.

Section 2:
The Common Defense Fund
4 Department of Defense
by Christopher Miller

- *A Cautionary Tale*

Citizens of the world, brace yourselves, because what you ae about to hear will send shivers down your spine. "The Common Defense Fund: Department of Defense" by Christopher Miller is a deeply unsettling manifesto on reconfiguring America's military might to fit a narrowly defined vision of national security. Miller, a former Acting Secretary of Defense under President Trump, uses this document to outline a plan that prioritizes aggressive defense strategies, significant budget reallocations, and a shift in focus towards perceived immediate threats, all while potentially undermining long-term stability and global cooperation.

Miller begins by arguing for a substantial increase in defense spending, asserting that current levels are insufficient to meet the growing threats from global adversaries. This call for increased military expenditure comes at a time when other critical areas like healthcare, education, and infrastructure are in dire need of funding. The prioritization of defense over these essential services raises serious ethical and practical questions about the allocation of national resources. Miller advocates for a more aggressive stance on global military engagement. He proposes increasing the number of U.S. military bases around the world and enhancing the country's ability to project power in key strategic regions. While he frames this as a necessary measure to counter global threats, such as China and Russia, it raises significant concerns about the potential for escalating tensions and provoking adversaries. This aggressive militarization strategy could lead to a new arms race, heightened global instability, and increased likelihood of military confrontations.

A core component of Miller's vision is the reallocation of funds within the Department of Defense to focus more on high-tech weaponry and cyber capabilities. While modernization is crucial, this emphasis risks neglecting other vital areas such as personnel training, veteran services, and maintenance of existing equipment. By channeling funds predominantly towards cutting-edge technologies, the plan could create imbalances that weaken overall military readiness and effectiveness.

Miller also advocates for a more aggressive stance in international relations, proposing a doctrine that favors pre-emptive strikes and unilateral actions. This hawkish approach risks escalating global tensions and alienating allies, undermining the collaborative efforts necessary for addressing shared security challenges. The potential for increased conflict and instability is a significant concern, as it could lead to a more dangerous and unpredictable world.

In his critique of current defense strategies, Miller calls for a reduction in what he terms "bureaucratic bloat" within the Pentagon. While efficiency improvements are always welcome, his proposed cuts could lead to the loss of essential oversight and support functions. This reduction in administrative capacity might hamper the Department's ability to manage complex operations effectively and maintain accountability. Miller's vision includes a controversial push to privatize certain military functions, arguing that the private sector can provide these services more efficiently. This privatization raises significant concerns about accountability, transparency, and the potential for conflicts of interest. History has shown that privatizing military functions often leads to higher costs and decreased control over essential operations, potentially compromising national security.

Another troubling aspect of Miller's plan is his stance on civil-military relations. He suggests a closer integration of military and civilian spheres, which could blur the lines between defense and domestic policy. This integration risks politicizing the military, undermining its apolitical stance, and eroding the trust that is crucial for its effective functioning within a democratic society.

In summary, "The Common Defense Fund: Department of Defense" by Christopher Miller presents a vision for the future of American defense that is fraught with risks and ethical dilemmas. His call for increased military spending, aggressive international postures, and privatization of military functions raises significant concerns about the long-term implications for national security and global stability. Miller's prioritizing militaristic strategies, driven by a narrow view of immediate threats, neglect the broader, more complex challenges that require inclusive security policies and cooperative approaches.

Why We Can't Trust Christopher Miller

We cannot trust Christopher Miller because his background and actions reveal a penchant for prioritizing aggressive military strategies and political loyalty over balanced and thoughtful defense policies. As a former Acting Secretary of Defense under President Trump, Miller's tenure was marked by controversial decisions, including the abrupt reduction of U.S. troops in Afghanistan and Iraq, which many experts criticized for destabilizing these regions and compromising long-term strategic goals. His rushed actions were seen as politically motivated, aimed at fulfilling campaign promises rather than ensuring national security, demonstrating a troubling disregard for the complexities of international engagement.

Miller's close ties to Trump and his role in the post-election transition period further erode trust. He was appointed to his position shortly after the 2020 presidential election, a move widely perceived as an effort to install loyalists in key defense roles during a tumultuous political period. His involvement in the delayed response to the January 6th Capitol riot also raises serious questions about his judgment and commitment to democratic principles. This delay in deploying the National Guard, despite clear and present danger, underscores a troubling alignment with political interests over the safety and stability of the nation. This incident alone casts a long shadow over his reliability and decision-making capabilities.

Moreover, Miller's push for privatizing military functions and reducing bureaucratic oversight within the Pentagon suggests a disregard for accountability and transparency. Privatization can lead to conflicts of interest and higher costs, while reducing oversight risks weakening the Department of Defense's ability to manage complex operations effectively. These aspects of Miller's background highlight a track record of decisions that favor short-term, politically expedient outcomes over the long-term integrity and security of the nation's defense infrastructure. His tenure exemplifies how political motivates can undermine the principles of responsible governance and national security, making him a figure whose actions warrant deep skepticism and distrust.

Section 2:
The Common Defense Fund
5 Department of Homeland Security
by Ken Cuccinelli

- A Cautionary Tale

Friends, prepare yourselves; the tale you are about to hear will haunt your dreams. "The Common Defense Fund: Department of Homeland Security" by Kevin Cuccinelli is a deeply upsetting guide for transforming America's approach to national security. Cuccinelli, a former senior official in the Trump administration, outlines a vision that prioritizes aggressive enforcement and restrictive policies over balanced, humane, and effective security measures. His proposals reveal a commitment to a hardline stance that will undermine civil liberties and strain the fabric of American democracy.

Cuccinelli begins by advocating for significant increases in funding for border security and immigration enforcement. He argues that these measures are essential to protect the nation from external threats, but this perspective overlooks the complex realities of immigration and the human rights implications of such an approach. The emphasis on building walls and deploying more agents at the border reflects a simplistic and punitive view of immigration that fails to address root causes or consider the contributions of immigrants to American society.

A major component of Cuccinelli's plan involves expanding the use of detention for undocumented immigrants. He suggests increasing the capacity of detention centers and expediting deportation processes. This approach raises serious ethical concerns about the treatment of individuals in detention, many of whom are fleeing violence and persecution. The focus on detention and deportation risks violating international human rights standards and exacerbating the suffering of vulnerable populations.

Cuccinelli also calls for a more robust and intrusive surveillance system to monitor potential threats within the country. He advocates for increased data collection and enhanced cooperation between federal and local law enforcement agencies. This strategy threatens to erode privacy rights and civil liberties. The potential for abuse and discrimination in the application of such measures is high, particularly against minority communities.

The document outlines a strategy for strengthening the legal framework to support these aggressive policies. Cuccinelli proposes legislative changes to make it easier to detain and deport individuals and to expand the powers of immigration enforcement agencies. Such legal reforms could undermine due process and the rule of law, leading to a more authoritarian and less accountable government. The emphasis on legal mechanisms to facilitate enforcement over protections for individuals reflects a one-sided approach to security.

Another troubling aspect of Cuccinelli's vision is his stance on refugee and asylum policies. He advocates for stricter criteria and more rigorous vetting processes, arguing that this will prevent potential security threats. However, this approach ignores the humanitarian obligations of the United States and risks turning away individuals in desperate need of protection. The proposed policies could lead to a significant decrease in the number of refugees and asylum seekers admitted to the country, undermining America's long-standing tradition of offering refuge to those in need.

Cuccinelli's focus on enhancing emergency response capabilities also takes a concerning turn. While improving disaster response is crucial, his proposals prioritize a militarized approach that could marginalize civilian agencies and local communities. The emphasis on federal control and military involvement in disaster response risks undermining community-based efforts and the essential role of local authorities in managing crises effectively.

In summary, "The Common Defense Fund: Department of Homeland Security" by Kevin Cuccinelli presents a vision for national security that is fraught with ethical dilemmas and potential risks to civil liberties. His call for increased enforcement, expanded detention, and enhanced surveillance reflects a hardline approach that prioritizes punitive measures over balanced, humane, and effective security strategies. Cuccinelli's proposals, neglect the broader, more complex challenges that require comprehensive and inclusive policies.

Why We Can't Trust Kevin Cuccinelli

We cannot trust Kevin Cuccinelli because his background and actions reveal a consistent pattern of extreme policies and controversial decisions that prioritize enforcement and control over humanitarian and democratic principles. As Virginia's Attorney General, his tenure was marked by aggressive attacks on science and reproductive rights. He sued the EPA over its finding that greenhouse gases are a danger to public health, showing a blatant disregard for climate science, including an attack on a prominent scientist at the University of Virginia, that was ultimately thrown out of Virginia Supreme Court.

As a former acting director of U.S. Citizenship and Immigration Services (USCIS) and senior official in the Trump administration, Cuccinelli's tenure was marked by aggressive immigration enforcement measures. He implemented policies that significantly restricted asylum seekers, reduced refugee admissions, and expanded the use of detention for undocumented immigrants. These actions reflected a hardline stance that often disregarded human rights and due process.

Cuccinelli's role in pushing for public charge rule changes, which made it more difficult for immigrants to obtain green cards if they were deemed likely to use public benefits, further highlights his punitive approach. This rule was criticized for targeting low-income immigrants and discouraging them from seeking essential services. His actions demonstrated a willingness to prioritize a narrow, punitive vision of immigration policy over the well-being and integration of immigrant communities. This track record raises serious concerns about his commitment to fair and humane governance.

Moreover, Cuccinelli's involvement in expanding surveillance and cooperation between federal and local law enforcement agencies points to a troubling disregard for civil liberties. His support for increased data collection and intrusive monitoring measures threatens privacy rights and risks discrimination against minority communities. The potential for abuse in the application of these measures is high, reflecting a dangerous tilt towards authoritarianism. Cuccinelli's background and actions suggest a governance style that values control and enforcement over justice and human rights, making him a figure whose policies and intentions warrant deep skepticism and distrust.

Section 2:
The Common Defense Fund
6 Department of State
by Kiron K. Skinner

- A Cautionary Tale

Come closer, for the chilling account you are about to hear is not for the faint-hearted. "The Common Defense Fund: Department of State" by Kiron K. Skinner is a disconcerting blueprint for redefining America's role in international diplomacy. Skinner, a former Director of Policy Planning at the State Department, outlines a vision that emphasizes assertive and unilateral action, prioritizing national interests over collaborative global efforts. Her proposals suggest a shift away from traditional diplomacy towards a more confrontational and transactional approach to international relations.

Skinner begins by advocating for a significant increase in defense and security funding within the State Department. She argues that bolstering military capabilities is essential to protecting national interests, even within the realm of diplomacy. This emphasis on militarization risks overshadowing the diplomatic tools and soft power that have long been crucial to maintaining global stability and fostering international cooperation.

A core component of Skinner's strategy involves restructuring the State Department to align more closely with the administration's foreign policy agenda. She proposes appointing diplomats and officials who are staunchly committed to conservative principles and the current administration's goals. This focus on ideological alignment over diplomatic experience and expertise threatens to undermine the department's ability to effectively navigate complex international landscapes and build consensus among diverse global actors.

Skinner also calls for a more aggressive stance in dealing with international organizations and alliances. She advocates for reassessing and potentially withdrawing from multilateral agreements that do not directly benefit U.S. interests. This approach could lead to the erosion of long-standing alliances and partnerships, weakening the collective security frameworks that have historically helped to prevent global conflicts and fostered international cooperation.

In her critique of current diplomatic practices, Skinner emphasizes the need for a more transactional approach to foreign aid and international assistance. She suggests that aid should be strictly conditional on the recipient countries' alignment with U.S. policy objectives. This shift from humanitarian assistance to a quid-pro-quo model risks alienating allies and partners, reducing the effectiveness of U.S. foreign aid as a tool for promoting global stability and development.

Skinner's vision includes a robust information and propaganda strategy to influence public opinion both domestically and internationally. She recommends enhancing the State Department's capabilities in strategic communications to counter misinformation and promote the administration's narrative. While combating misinformation is important, the potential for this strategy to devolve into state-sponsored propaganda raises serious ethical and democratic concerns.

The document also outlines a plan to streamline and centralize decision-making processes within the State Department. Skinner argues that this will improve efficiency and ensure that diplomatic actions are tightly aligned with the administration's objectives. However, this centralization risks marginalizing the input of career diplomats and regional experts, leading to less informed and potentially more volatile foreign policy decisions.

In summary, "The Common Defense Fund: Department of State" by Kiron K. Skinner presents a vision for U.S. diplomacy that prioritizes military strength, ideological alignment, and transactional relationships over traditional diplomatic values. Her proposals for restructuring the State Department, reassessing international alliances, and implementing a robust propaganda strategy reflect a shift towards a more confrontational and unilateral foreign policy approach. Skinner's vision, driven by a narrow view of national interests, neglects the broader, more complex challenges that require comprehensive and cooperative diplomatic efforts. This document serves as a stern reminder of the potential dangers of prioritizing short-term gains and aggressive tactics over the long-term principles of diplomacy, global stability, and international cooperation.

Why We Can't Trust Kiron K. Skinner

We cannot trust Kiron K. Skinner because her background and actions reveal a commitment to an aggressive and unilateral approach to foreign policy that often undermines diplomatic norms and global cooperation. As a former Director of Policy Planning at the State Department under the Trump administration, Skinner was instrumental in crafting policies that prioritized military strength and nationalistic agendas over collaborative international relations. Her tenure was marked by a shift towards a more confrontational stance in foreign affairs, emphasizing the use of hard power and transactional diplomacy.

One notable example of Skinner's controversial approach is her advocacy for re-evaluating and potentially withdrawing from multilateral agreements and international organizations that she deemed insufficiently beneficial to U.S. interests. This stance jeopardized long-standing alliances and partnerships that have been crucial for maintaining global stability and addressing transnational challenges. Skinner's push for a more isolationist and self-serving foreign policy threatened to erode the collaborative frameworks essential for tackling issues such as climate change, global health, and international security.

Moreover, Skinner's vision for the State Department involved appointing diplomats and officials based on their ideological alignment with conservative principles, rather than their diplomatic experience and expertise. This focus on political loyalty over professional qualifications risks undermining the effectiveness of U.S. diplomacy. It can lead to a lack of nuanced understanding in international negotiations and diminish the department's capacity to build consensus among diverse global actors.

In summary, Kiron K. Skinner's history of prioritizing aggressive tactics, ideological alignment, and transactional diplomacy over cooperative and inclusive foreign policy efforts raises significant concerns about her approach to international relations. Her tenure at the State Department exemplifies how a narrow, confrontational vision can undermine the principles of diplomacy and global cooperation, making her a figure whose policies and intentions warrant deep skepticism and distrust.

Section 2:
The Common Defense Fund
7 Intelligence Community
by Dustin J. Carmack

- A Cautionary Tale

Listen up, folks, because what you are about to learn is deeply disturbing. "The Common Defense Fund: Intelligence Community" by Dustin J. Carmack is a deeply unsettling treatise on reshaping America's intelligence apparatus. Carmack, a former Chief of Staff to the Director of National Intelligence, outlines a vision that prioritizes aggressive intelligence gathering and operational secrecy over transparency and accountability. His proposals reflect a drive to expand the powers and reach of the intelligence community (IC), raising concerns about civil liberties and democratic oversight.

Carmack begins by advocating for increased funding and resources for the intelligence community, arguing that current levels are insufficient to meet the complex and evolving threats faced by the United States. While enhancing capabilities is crucial, the emphasis on unchecked growth risks fostering an environment where surveillance and intelligence operations can proceed with minimal oversight. This could lead to abuses of power and encroachments on individual privacy and freedoms, eroding the trust and accountability essential in a democratic society.

A core component of Carmack's strategy involves enhancing cybersecurity and counterintelligence efforts. He proposes aggressive measures to protect national security from cyber threats, including expanded monitoring and data collection on both domestic and international fronts. This approach, while addressing legitimate security concerns, also raises the specter of mass surveillance and the potential for significant intrusions into the private lives of citizens. The balance between security and privacy is precarious, and Carmack's vision appears to lean heavily towards the former at the expense of the latter.

Carmack also calls for greater operational secrecy within the intelligence community. He argues that transparency can hinder the effectiveness of intelligence operations and proposes measures to limit the dissemination of information both within the IC and to the public. This focus on secrecy undermines democratic oversight and accountability, which are essential for ensuring that intelligence activities are conducted lawfully and ethically. The potential for unchecked power and secretive operations is deeply alarming in a democratic society.

Another troubling aspect of Carmack's vision is his stance on expanding the IC's influence over domestic affairs. He advocates for closer collaboration between intelligence agencies and domestic law enforcement to counter threats such as terrorism and cybercrime. While cooperation is necessary, blurring the lines between foreign intelligence and domestic law enforcement risks eroding civil liberties and increasing the potential for surveillance abuses against American citizens. The delicate balance between protecting the nation and preserving individual rights is at risk in Carmack's approach.

Carmack's document also suggests significant legal reforms to empower the intelligence community further. He proposes changes that would streamline the process for obtaining surveillance warrants and reduce the checks and balances currently in place. Such reforms could weaken judicial oversight and increase the likelihood of intrusive surveillance practices, undermining the legal protections meant to safeguard individual rights. The shift toward empowering the IC with fewer constraints raises alarming questions about the potential for unchecked authority and misuse of power.

In summary, "The Common Defense Fund: Intelligence Community" by Dustin J. Carmack presents a vision for expanding and empowering America's intelligence apparatus in ways that pose serious risks to civil liberties and democratic governance. His call for increased funding, operational secrecy, and enhanced surveillance capabilities reflects a prioritization of security over transparency and accountability. Carmack's proposals, driven by a desire to address evolving threats, neglect the essential balance between protecting national security and preserving individual freedoms. This document serves as a warning of the potential dangers of unchecked intelligence powers and the erosion of democratic oversight. It underscores the need for vigilance in maintaining the principles of transparency, accountability, and respect for civil liberties within the intelligence community.

Why We Can't Trust Dustin K. Carmack

We cannot trust Dustin J. Carmack because his background and actions reveal a consistent pattern of prioritizing aggressive intelligence measures and operational secrecy over transparency and accountability. As a former Chief of Staff to the Director of National Intelligence, Carmack played a significant role in shaping policies that expanded the reach and power of the intelligence community (IC). His tenure was marked by a push for increased surveillance capabilities and reduced oversight, which raise significant concerns about the potential for abuses of power and violations of civil liberties.

One notable example of Carmack's troubling approach is his advocacy for enhanced cybersecurity and counterintelligence efforts that involve extensive monitoring and data collection. While these measures are justified as necessary for national security, they also pave the way for mass surveillance and intrusion into the private lives of citizens. During his time in the intelligence community, Carmack supported initiatives that blurred the lines between foreign intelligence and domestic law enforcement, increasing the risk of surveillance abuses against American citizens. This approach reflects a disregard for the delicate balance between security and privacy, prioritizing the former at the expense of the latter.

Moreover, Carmack's emphasis on operational secrecy within the IC is deeply concerning. He has argued that transparency can hinder intelligence effectiveness and has supported measures to limit information dissemination both within the IC and to the public. This stance undermines democratic oversight and accountability, which are crucial for ensuring that intelligence activities are conducted lawfully and ethically. Carmack's background and actions suggest a governance style that values unchecked intelligence operations over the principles of transparency and accountability, making him a figure whose policies and intentions warrant deep skepticism and distrust. His vision of an empowered, secretive intelligence community poses significant risks to civil liberties and democratic governance. Carmack's approach, including his endorsement of a dangerous expansion of presidential authority under unitary executive theory, further increases the risk of authoritarian rule by eroding the role of Congress and the judiciary in safeguarding democratic processes. Opting instead for a presidential reign, like a king or monarchy.

Section 2:
The Common Defense Fund
8 Media Agencies: U.S. Agency for Global Media
by Mora Namdar

- A Cautionary Tale

Pay close attention, everyone, because this next story is unbelievably frightening. "The Common Defense Fund: Media Agencies U.S. Agency for Global Media" by Mora Namdar is a disconcerting blueprint for reshaping America's global media strategy. Namdar, with her background in conservative media policy, outlines a vision that emphasizes ideological conformity and strategic messaging over journalistic independence and balanced reporting. Her proposals reflect a drive to use media as a tool for political influence, raising significant concerns about the erosion of free press principles and democratic accountability.

Namdar begins by advocating for a substantial increase in funding and resources for the U.S. Agency for Global Media (USAGM). She argues that enhancing America's global media capabilities is essential for countering foreign propaganda and promoting U.S. interests abroad. While strengthening global media outreach is important, Namdar's emphasis on using media as a strategic weapon risks turning the USAGM into a propaganda machine, rather than a source of reliable and unbiased information.

A core component of Namdar's strategy involves restructuring the leadership and operations of USAGM to ensure alignment with conservative values and the administration's foreign policy goals. She proposes appointing leaders who are ideologically committed to these principles and can steer the agency's content accordingly. This focus on ideological alignment over journalistic independence threatens to undermine the credibility and effectiveness of U.S. global media efforts. It risks transforming the USAGM into an echo chamber that serves political interests rather than informing and educating international audiences.

Namdar also calls for an aggressive approach to countering foreign media narratives. She advocates for proactive measures to discredit and counteract propaganda from adversarial nations. While countering disinformation is crucial, the methods proposed by Namdar could lead to a tit-for-tat media war that escalates tensions and reduces the overall quality of global discourse. Her vision emphasizes confrontation over cooperation, which could further polarize international relations and undermine efforts to foster mutual understanding and dialogue.

In her critique of current media strategies, Namdar emphasizes the need for more assertive and coordinated messaging. She suggests creating a centralized command within the USAGM to oversee and direct all media operations, ensuring consistency and effectiveness in promoting U.S. interests. This centralization risks stifling diversity of thought and editorial independence, crucial elements for a vibrant and credible media environment. The potential for top-down control over content raises serious ethical concerns about the manipulation of information and the suppression of dissenting views.

Another troubling aspect of Namdar's vision is her stance on using media to influence domestic audiences. She advocates for leveraging USAGM's resources to shape public opinion within the United States, particularly on issues related to national security and foreign policy. This blurring of lines between foreign and domestic media operations raises concerns about the misuse of public resources and the potential for government propaganda to influence domestic politics. It threatens the fundamental principles of a free and independent press that are essential for a healthy democracy.

In summary, "The Common Defense Fund: Media Agencies U.S. Agency for Global Media" by Mora Namdar presents a vision for U.S. global media that prioritizes ideological conformity, aggressive messaging, and centralized control. Her proposals for restructuring USAGM leadership, countering foreign narratives, and influencing domestic audiences reflect a troubling shift towards using media as a tool for political influence. Namdar's vision, driven by a desire to promote conservative values and U.S. interests, neglects the broader principles of journalistic integrity and free press. This document serves as a caution of the potential dangers of politicizing media agencies and eroding democratic accountability. It underscores the need to preserve the independence and credibility of global media efforts to maintain trust and integrity in international discourse.

Why We Can't Trust Mora Namdar

We cannot trust Mora Namdar because her background and actions reveal a commitment to using media as a tool for political influence, often at the expense of journalistic integrity and balanced reporting. As a former senior advisor at the U.S. Agency for Global Media (USAGM) and a proponent of conservative media policies, Namdar has been instrumental in pushing for a restructuring of media agencies to align with ideological goals. Her tenure was marked by efforts to centralize control over media operations and ensure that content aligned with conservative values, reflecting a partisan approach that prioritizes ideological conformity over factual reporting.

One notable example of Namdar's troubling approach is her advocacy for appointing leaders within USAGM who are ideologically committed to conservative principles and the administration's foreign policy goals. This focus on political loyalty over journalistic independence threatens the credibility and effectiveness of U.S. global media efforts. Namdar's push for centralizing control over media operations and ensuring consistent messaging across all platforms risks turning USAGM into an echo chamber that serves political interests rather than informing and educating international audiences. Her actions indicate a willingness to sacrifice the foundational principles of journalistic integrity for the sake of promoting a specific political agenda.

Moreover, Namdar's stance on leveraging USAGM resources to influence domestic audiences raises significant ethical concerns. She advocates for using government-funded media to shape public opinion within the United States on national security and foreign policy issues, blurring the lines between foreign and domestic media operations. This approach risks the misuse of public resources and the potential for government propaganda to manipulate domestic politics. Namdar's background and actions suggest a governance style that values political loyalty and ideological conformity over the principles of a free and independent press, making her a figure whose policies and intentions warrant deep skepticism and distrust. Her vision for media agencies undermines the essential elements of journalistic integrity and democratic accountability, posing significant risks to the health of public discourse and the functioning of a free society.

Section 2:
The Common Defense Fund
8 Media Agencies: Corporation for Public Broadcasting
by Mike Gonzalez

- A Cautionary Tale

Gather 'round, all, for the events you are about to hear are truly
nightmarish. "The Common Defense Fund: Media Agencies
Corporation for Public Broadcasting" by Mike Gonzalez is a
profoundly unsettling blueprint for reshaping America's public
broadcasting landscape. Gonzalez, a former senior fellow at the
Heritage Foundation and a staunch advocate for conservative media
reform, outlines a vision that prioritizes ideological conformity and
political messaging over journalistic independence and balanced
reporting. His proposals reflect a drive to transform public
broadcasting into a tool for advancing conservative agendas, raising
significant concerns about the erosion of free press principles.

Gonzalez begins by advocating for a substantial overhaul of the
Corporation for Public Broadcasting (CPB). He argues that the
current structure is biased and fails to adequately represent
conservative viewpoints. His solution is to restructure the leadership
and operations of CPB to ensure alignment with conservative values
and the administration's policy goals. This focus on ideological
alignment over journalistic integrity threatens to undermine the
credibility and effectiveness of public broadcasting. It risks turning
CPB into a partisan platform that serves political interests rather than
informing and educating the public.

A core component of Gonzalez's strategy involves increasing oversight
and control over the content produced by public broadcasting entities
such as PBS and NPR. He proposes appointing leaders who are
ideologically committed to conservative principles and can steer
programming accordingly. This approach risks stifling editorial
independence and reducing the diversity of perspectives presented to
the public. Gonzalez's vision emphasizes a top-down control that
could marginalize dissenting voices and promote a homogenized,
politically driven narrative.

Gonzalez also calls for a more aggressive approach to countering what he perceives as liberal bias in public broadcasting. He advocates for proactive measures to balance programming by increasing conservative content and viewpoints. While promoting diverse perspectives is important, the methods proposed by Gonzalez could lead to an imbalanced and politically charged media environment. His focus on counteracting perceived bias rather than fostering genuine diversity of thought risks further polarizing public discourse and undermining trust in public media.

In his critique of current public broadcasting practices, Gonzalez emphasizes the need for more stringent accountability measures. He suggests implementing rigorous performance evaluations and funding reviews to ensure that public broadcasting entities adhere to conservative values. This emphasis on accountability, while seemingly reasonable, masks an agenda to impose political conformity and control over public media. The potential for using funding as leverage to enforce ideological compliance is a significant threat to the independence and autonomy of public broadcasters.

Gonzalez's proposals also include leveraging public broadcasting to influence domestic audiences on issues related to national security and foreign policy. This blurring of lines between public service media and government propaganda raises serious ethical concerns. The potential for government influence over public broadcasting content threatens the fundamental principles of a free and independent press, essential for a healthy democracy.

In summary, "The Common Defense Fund: Media Agencies Corporation for Public Broadcasting" by Mike Gonzalez presents a vision for U.S. public broadcasting that prioritizes ideological conformity, political messaging, and privatization. His proposals for restructuring CPB leadership, increasing content oversight, and influencing domestic audiences reflect a troubling shift towards using public media as a tool for advancing conservative agendas. Gonzalez's vision neglects the broader principles of journalistic integrity and free press. This document serves as a bleak reminder of the potential dangers of politicizing public media and eroding democratic accountability. It underscores the need to preserve the independence and credibility of public broadcasting to maintain trust and integrity in public discourse.

Why We Can't Trust Mike Gonzalez

We cannot trust Mike Gonzalez because his background and actions reveal a consistent pattern of prioritizing ideological conformity and political messaging over journalistic integrity and balanced reporting. As a former senior fellow at the Heritage Foundation, Gonzalez has been a vocal advocate for conservative media policies, pushing for restructuring media agencies to align with conservative goals. His tenure at the Heritage Foundation was marked by efforts to promote conservative narratives and discredit opposing viewpoints.

One notable example of Gonzalez's controversial approach is his advocacy for transforming the Corporation for Public Broadcasting (CPB). He has proposed restructuring CPB's leadership to ensure alignment with conservative values, thereby undermining its independence. This focus on ideological loyalty over journalistic independence threatens the credibility and effectiveness of public broadcasting. Gonzalez's push for increased oversight and control over content risks turning CPB into a partisan platform that serves political interests rather than informing and educating the public.

Moreover, Gonzalez's stance on leveraging public broadcasting resources to influence domestic audiences raises significant ethical concerns. He advocates for using government-funded media to shape public opinion on national security and foreign policy issues, blurring the lines between public service media and government propaganda. This approach risks the misuse of public resources and the potential for government influence over public broadcasting content, undermining the principles of a free and independent press essential for a healthy democracy.

Gonzalez's vision for public broadcasting, marked by his efforts to centralize control and promote conservative content, reflects a governance style that values political loyalty and ideological conformity over the principles of journalistic integrity and balanced reporting. His background and actions suggest a willingness to sacrifice the foundational elements of free press for the sake of advancing a specific political agenda. His vision undermines the essential elements of journalistic independence and democratic accountability, posing significant risks to the health of public discourse and the functioning of a free society.

Section 2:
The Common Defense Fund
9 Agency for International Development
by Max Primorac

- A Cautionary Tale

Alright, everyone, hold tight, because what you are about to hear will chill you to the bone. "The Common Defense: Agency for International Development" by Max Primorac is a deeply troubling manifesto on reshaping America's approach to international aid and development. Primorac, a former senior official at USAID, outlines a vision that prioritizes strategic interests and ideological conformity over humanitarian principles and global cooperation. His proposals reflect a drive to use development aid as a tool for political leverage, raising significant concerns about the erosion of the fundamental goals of international development.

Primorac begins by advocating for a substantial increase in funding for strategic aid initiatives. He argues that current levels are insufficient to meet the geopolitical challenges faced by the United States. While enhancing aid capabilities is crucial, Primorac's emphasis on strategic interests risks turning aid into a mere extension of foreign policy, rather than a means to alleviate poverty and foster sustainable development. This approach could undermine the core mission of USAID, which is to promote global development and humanitarian assistance.

A core component of Primorac's strategy involves restructuring USAID to align more closely with the administration's foreign policy objectives. He proposes appointing leaders who are ideologically committed to these principles and can steer the agency's programs accordingly. This focus on ideological alignment over expertise and experience threatens to undermine the effectiveness and credibility of USAID. It risks transforming the agency into a politically driven entity that serves strategic interests rather than addressing global development challenges.

Primorac also calls for an aggressive approach to using aid as a tool for political leverage. He advocates for conditional aid programs that require recipient countries to align with U.S. policy objectives. While conditionality can sometimes ensure aid effectiveness, Primorac's approach risks coercing vulnerable countries into adopting policies that may not be in their best interest. This could lead to resentment and undermine the long-term relationships necessary for effective development cooperation.

In his critique of current aid practices, Primorac emphasizes the need for more stringent oversight and accountability measures. He suggests implementing rigorous performance evaluations and funding reviews to ensure that aid programs adhere to strategic goals. While accountability is important, his emphasis on control and oversight masks an agenda to impose political conformity and control over aid programs.

Another troubling aspect of Primorac's vision is his stance on privatizing certain functions of USAID. He argues that privatization would reduce costs and increase efficiency. However, this approach risks compromising the public service mission of USAID and turning it into a profit-driven enterprise. Privatization could lead to reduced access to essential services for the most vulnerable populations and a focus on commercially viable projects over humanitarian and development needs.

Primorac's proposals also include leveraging development aid to influence domestic audiences on issues related to national security and foreign policy. This blurring of lines between development assistance and government propaganda raises serious ethical concerns. The potential for government influence over aid programs threatens the fundamental principles of impartiality and neutrality that are essential for effective humanitarian assistance.

In summary, "The Common Defense: Agency for International Development" by Max Primorac presents a vision for U.S. international aid that prioritizes strategic interests, political leverage, and privatization. His proposals for restructuring USAID leadership, increasing oversight, and influencing domestic audiences reflect a troubling shift towards using development aid as a tool for advancing political agendas. Primorac's vision neglects the broader principles of humanitarianism and global cooperation. This document serves as a reminder of the potential dangers of politicizing international aid and eroding the fundamental goals of global development.

Why We Can't Trust Max Primorac

We cannot trust Max Primorac because his background and actions reveal a consistent pattern of prioritizing political leverage and strategic interests over the fundamental goals of humanitarian aid and global development. As a former senior official at USAID, Primorac has a history of promoting policies that align development aid closely with U.S. foreign policy objectives, often at the expense of the core mission of alleviating poverty and fostering sustainable development. His tenure was marked by efforts to use aid as a tool for advancing geopolitical agendas, reflecting a governance style that values political conformity over effective humanitarian assistance.

One notable example of Primorac's controversial approach is his advocacy for conditional aid programs that require recipient countries to align with U.S. policy objectives. While conditionality can sometimes ensure aid effectiveness, Primorac's method risks coercing vulnerable countries into adopting policies that may not be in their best interest. This approach undermines the long-term relationships necessary for effective development cooperation and can lead to resentment among recipient nations. Primorac's focus on political leverage over genuine development goals raises serious ethical concerns about the manipulation of aid for strategic purposes.

Moreover, Primorac's stance on privatizing certain functions of USAID further highlights his problematic approach. He argues that privatization would reduce costs and increase efficiency, but this perspective risks compromising the public service mission of USAID. Privatization could turn development aid into a profit-driven enterprise, reducing access to essential services for the most vulnerable populations and prioritizing commercially viable projects over humanitarian needs. Primorac's background and actions suggest a willingness to sacrifice the core principles of impartiality and neutrality that are essential for effective humanitarian assistance, making him a figure whose policies and intentions warrant deep skepticism and distrust. His vision for international aid poses significant risks to the integrity and effectiveness of global development efforts.

Section 3:
The General Welfare
10 Department of Agriculture
by Daren Bakst

- A Cautionary Tale

Folks, take a deep breath, because what you are about to hear will leave you in shock. "The General Welfare: Department of Agriculture" by Daren Bakst is a deeply unsettling treatise on reshaping America's agricultural policies. Bakst, a senior research fellow at the Heritage Foundation, outlines a vision that prioritizes deregulation, free-market principles, and reduced government intervention over the well-being of farmers and consumers. His proposals reflect a drive to transform the Department of Agriculture (USDA) into an entity that serves corporate interests, raising significant concerns about the erosion of support for small farmers and sustainable agricultural practices.

Bakst begins by advocating for significant cuts to agricultural subsidies and support programs. He argues that these programs distort the market and encourage dependency. While reducing waste and inefficiency is important, Bakst's approach risks undermining the stability of small farms that rely on these supports to survive. His focus on market-driven policies overlooks the complex challenges faced by family-owned farms and rural communities, potentially leading to increased consolidation in the agricultural sector and the demise of small, independent farms.

A core component of Bakst's strategy involves extensive deregulation. He proposes rolling back numerous environmental and safety regulations, arguing that they impose unnecessary burdens on farmers. While reducing regulatory burdens can spur innovation, Bakst's aggressive deregulation agenda threatens to compromise environmental protections and food safety standards. This could lead to increased pollution, degradation of natural resources, and greater risks to public health, as the drive for profit overrides the need for sustainable and safe agricultural practices.

Bakst also calls for privatizing many functions currently managed by the USDA. He suggests that the private sector can provide these services more efficiently and cost-effectively. However, this approach risks prioritizing profit over public good. Privatization could result in reduced access to essential services for small farmers, particularly those in remote or underserved areas, and diminish the USDA's ability to address public health concerns, food security, and rural development comprehensively.

He advocates for reducing the role of government in agriculture and allowing market forces to dictate production and distribution. This laissez-faire philosophy ignores the unique vulnerabilities of the agricultural sector, including its susceptibility to weather, pests, and market fluctuations. Without adequate support and intervention, many farmers could be left to struggle or fail, exacerbating economic inequalities and threatening food security.

Another troubling aspect of Bakst's vision is his stance on trade policies. He supports removing trade barriers and promoting free trade agreements, arguing that they benefit American farmers. While trade can open new markets, Bakst's approach risks exposing farmers to volatile global markets and unfair competition from countries with lower labor and environmental standards. This could lead to a race to the bottom, where cost-cutting measures compromise worker rights, environmental sustainability, and product quality.

Bakst's proposals also include reducing funding for nutrition programs, such as SNAP, which provides critical support to low-income families. He argues that these programs are prone to abuse and create dependency. However, cutting these programs would disproportionately affect vulnerable populations, increasing food insecurity and poverty. It reflects a lack of understanding or concern for the social safety nets that support millions of Americans.

In summary, "The General Welfare: Department of Agriculture" by Daren Bakst presents a vision for U.S. agriculture that prioritizes deregulation, free-market principles, and reduced government intervention. His proposals for cutting subsidies, extensive deregulation, privatization, and reducing support for nutrition programs reflect a troubling shift towards serving corporate interests over the needs of farmers and consumers. Bakst's vision neglects the broader principles of sustainability, equity, and public welfare.

Why We Can't Trust Daren Bakst

We cannot trust Daren Bakst because his background and actions reveal a consistent pattern of prioritizing deregulation and corporate interests over the well-being of farmers, consumers, and the environment. As a senior research fellow at the Heritage Foundation, Bakst has been a vocal advocate for free-market policies and reduced government intervention in agriculture. His tenure at the Heritage Foundation was marked by efforts to roll back environmental regulations, cut agricultural subsidies, and privatize key functions of the Department of Agriculture (USDA). This approach reflects a governance style that values market forces over the support and protection needed for sustainable agriculture and rural communities.

One notable example of Bakst's controversial approach is his advocacy for extensive deregulation in the agricultural sector. He has proposed rolling back numerous environmental and safety regulations, arguing that they impose unnecessary burdens on farmers. While reducing regulatory burdens can spur innovation, Bakst's aggressive deregulation agenda threatens to compromise environmental protections and food safety standards. His push for deregulation overlooks the potential for increased pollution, degradation of natural resources, and risks to public health, as profit-driven motives overshadow the need for sustainable and safe agricultural practices.

Moreover, Bakst's stance on cutting agricultural subsidies and support programs further highlights his problematic approach. He argues that these programs distort the market and encourage dependency, but this perspective fails to recognize the complex challenges faced by small farms. His focus on market-driven policies risks undermining the stability of family-owned farms that rely on these supports to survive. By advocating for a reduction in government intervention and support, Bakst's policies could lead to increased consolidation in the agricultural sector, threatening the viability of small, independent farms and exacerbating economic inequalities in rural communities. His background and actions suggest a willingness to sacrifice the well-being of farmers and consumers for the sake of free-market principles, making his policies and intentions deeply worrisome and untrustworthy.

Section 3:
The General Welfare
11 Department of Education
by Lindsey M. Burke

- A Cautionary Tale

Lean in, friends, because the story you are about to hear will make
your skin crawl. "The General Welfare: Department of Education" by
Lindsey M. Burke is a deeply troubling manifesto on reshaping
America's educational system. Burke, a prominent figure at the
Heritage Foundation, outlines a vision that prioritizes school choice,
deregulation, and reduced federal oversight over equity and access to
quality education for all. Her proposals reflect a drive to transform the
Department of Education into an entity that serves conservative
ideological goals, raising significant concerns about the erosion of
public education and the widening of educational disparities.

Burke begins by advocating for a substantial shift towards school
choice initiatives, such as vouchers and charter schools. She argues
that these programs empower parents and foster competition, leading
to improved educational outcomes. While school choice can offer
benefits, Burke's approach risks diverting critical funding away from
public schools, undermining their ability to serve all students. This
focus on privatization overlooks the essential role of public education
in providing equitable opportunities, potentially exacerbating
disparities and leaving the most vulnerable students behind.

A core component of Burke's strategy involves extensive deregulation
of the educational sector. She proposes rolling back numerous federal
regulations that she claims stifle innovation and local control. While
reducing bureaucratic red tape can be beneficial, Burke's aggressive
deregulation agenda threatens to eliminate safeguards that ensure
educational quality and protect students' rights. This could lead to a
fragmented system where educational standards vary widely,
compromising the overall quality of education and widening the gap
between affluent and disadvantaged communities.

Burke also calls for significantly reducing the federal government's
role in education, advocating for more control to be handed to states
and local authorities. She argues that local control allows for more

tailored and effective educational solutions. However, this approach risks creating a patchwork of educational standards and resources, where the quality of education a child receives is heavily dependent on their zip code. This decentralization can lead to significant inequalities, as states with fewer resources may struggle to provide the same level of education as wealthier states.

In her critique of current educational policies, Burke emphasizes the need for a free-market approach to education. She advocates for reducing the role of government and allowing market forces to dictate educational offerings. This laissez-faire philosophy ignores the unique challenges faced by public education, including its mission to serve all students, regardless of their socioeconomic background. Without adequate support and intervention, many schools, particularly those in disadvantaged areas, could struggle or fail, exacerbating educational inequalities.

Burke suggests that market mechanisms, rather than federal oversight, should drive school performance. This approach risks reducing accountability for educational outcomes and allows poorly performing schools to continue operating without necessary improvements. The lack of rigorous oversight could lead to a decline in educational standards and outcomes, particularly for vulnerable populations.

Burke's proposals also include reducing funding for federal education programs, such as Title I, which provides financial assistance to schools with high numbers of low-income students. Cutting these programs would disproportionately affect the most disadvantaged students, increasing educational inequities and undermining efforts to provide a high-quality education for all.

In summary, "The General Welfare: Department of Education" by Lindsey M. Burke presents a vision for U.S. education that prioritizes school choice, deregulation, and reduced federal oversight. Her proposals for shifting towards privatization, extensive deregulation, and reducing support for federal education programs reflect a troubling shift towards serving conservative ideological goals over the needs of all students. This document serves as a stark reminder of the potential dangers of prioritizing market-driven approaches over the fundamental goals of public education, underscoring the need to preserve a balanced and supportive educational policy.

Why We Can't Trust Lindsey M. Burke

We cannot trust Lindsey M. Burke because her background and actions reveal a consistent pattern of prioritizing conservative ideological goals and market-driven approaches over the fundamental principles of equity and access in education. As the director of the Center for Education Policy at the Heritage Foundation, Burke has been a vocal advocate for school choice initiatives, extensive deregulation, and reduced federal oversight. Her tenure at the Heritage Foundation was marked by efforts to promote policies that divert funding from public schools to private and charter schools, reflecting a governance style that values privatization over the support and protection of public education.

One notable example of Burke's controversial approach is her advocacy for school vouchers and charter schools. She argues that these programs empower parents and foster competition, but this perspective fails to recognize the critical role public schools play in providing equitable educational opportunities for all students. By diverting funds away from public schools, Burke's policies risk undermining their ability to serve disadvantaged communities, exacerbating educational disparities. Her focus on privatization overlooks the complex challenges faced by public schools, particularly those in underfunded areas, and threatens to leave the most vulnerable students behind.

Moreover, Burke's stance on extensive deregulation further highlights her problematic approach. She has proposed rolling back numerous federal regulations that ensure educational quality and protect students' rights, arguing that they stifle innovation and local control. However, her push for deregulation risks creating a fragmented educational system with widely varying standards and resources. This could compromise the overall quality of education and widen the gap between affluent and disadvantaged communities. Between private charter schools and the defunding of public schools, Burke, in effect, is advocating for the elimination of all public education. Am uneducated or "Christian" educated populace is easier to control and fits their agenda of theocratic takeover writ large. Burke's background and actions suggest a willingness to sacrifice the core principles of equity and access for the sake of conservative ideological goals, making her policies and intentions deeply concerning and untrustworthy.

Section 3:
The General Welfare
12 Department Energy and Related Commissions
by Bernard I. McNamee

- A Cautionary Tale

Listen carefully, everyone, because the tale you are about to hear is utterly horrifying. "The General Welfare: Department of Energy & Related Commissions" by Bernard I. McNamee is a deeply troubling blueprint for reshaping America's energy policies. McNamee, a former member of the Federal Energy Regulatory Commission (FERC) and a senior fellow at the Texas Public Policy Foundation, outlines a vision that prioritizes deregulation, fossil fuels, and reduced government intervention over sustainable energy development and environmental protection. His proposals reflect a drive to transform the Department of Energy (DOE) into an entity that serves corporate interests, raising significant concerns about the eroding environmental safeguards and the long-term sustainability of energy policies.

McNamee begins by advocating for a significant rollback of regulations that he argues stifle energy production and economic growth. He proposes reducing the regulatory burden on the fossil fuel industry, claiming that it will unleash economic potential and secure energy independence. While reducing unnecessary regulations can spur innovation, McNamee's approach threatens to undermine crucial environmental protections. Deregulation risks increased pollution, higher carbon emissions, and greater ecological damage, compromising public health and accelerating climate change.

A core component of McNamee's strategy involves a substantial increase in support for fossil fuel industries. He argues that coal, oil, and natural gas are essential for maintaining energy reliability and affordability. This emphasis on fossil fuels overlooks the critical need to transition to cleaner, renewable energy sources to mitigate the impacts of climate change. McNamee's vision prioritizes short-term economic gains over the long-term health of the planet, ignoring the urgent need for a sustainable energy future. McNamee calls for reducing federal oversight and increasing state control over energy policies. While local control can lead to tailored solutions, this approach risks creating a patchwork of regulations that could weaken national standards and hinder progress towards a unified energy strategy. States with fewer resources and differing priorities may struggle to implement effective environmental protections and sustainable energy policies.

McNamee advocates for reducing the role of government and allowing market forces to dictate energy production and consumption. This laissez-faire philosophy ignores the externalities associated with energy production, such as environmental degradation and public health impacts. Without adequate regulation and oversight, the energy market may prioritize profits over sustainability and public welfare, leading to long-term negative consequences.

Another troubling aspect of McNamee's vision is his stance on renewable energy. He argues that renewable energy sources, such as wind and solar, are unreliable and cannot meet the nation's energy demands. This perspective undermines the significant advancements in renewable energy technologies and the potential for a diversified energy portfolio. McNamee's focus on fossil fuels at the expense of renewables threatens to stall progress towards a cleaner, more sustainable energy future.

McNamee's proposals also include reducing funding for energy research and development programs, such as those focused on renewable energy and energy efficiency. He argues that private industry is better suited to drive innovation without government intervention. However, cutting these programs would hinder the development of new technologies and slow the transition to a sustainable energy economy.

In summary, "The General Welfare: Department of Energy & Related Commissions" by Bernard I. McNamee presents a vision for U.S. energy policy that prioritizes deregulation, fossil fuels, and reduced federal oversight. His proposals for rolling back regulations, increasing support for fossil fuels, and reducing funding for renewable energy and energy efficiency programs reflect a troubling shift towards serving corporate interests over the needs of the environment and public health. This document serves as a necessary reminder of the potential dangers of prioritizing short-term economic gains over long-term sustainability, underscoring the need to preserve a balanced and forward-thinking energy policy.

Why We Can't Trust Bernard I. McNamee

We cannot trust Bernard I. McNamee because his background and actions reveal a consistent pattern of prioritizing deregulation and fossil fuel interests over environmental protection and sustainable energy development. As a former member of the Federal Energy Regulatory Commission (FERC) and a senior fellow at the Texas Public Policy Foundation, McNamee has been a vocal advocate for rolling back regulations that he claims stifle energy production and economic growth. His tenure at FERC was marked by efforts to reduce regulatory burdens on the fossil fuel industry, reflecting a governance style that values corporate interests over public health and environmental sustainability.

One notable example of McNamee's controversial approach is his support for increased fossil fuel production. He has argued that coal, oil, and natural gas are essential for maintaining energy reliability and affordability, dismissing the critical need to transition to renewable energy sources. This perspective overlooks the significant environmental and health impacts of fossil fuel consumption, including pollution and climate change. McNamee's focus on short-term economic gains at the expense of long-term sustainability highlights a troubling disregard for the urgent need to address the global climate crisis.

Moreover, McNamee's stance on reducing federal oversight in favor of state control further underscores his problematic approach. He claims that states are better equipped to manage their energy resources without federal interference, but this strategy risks creating a fragmented regulatory landscape with weakened national standards. States with fewer resources and differing priorities may struggle to implement effective environmental protections, leading to increased pollution and ecological degradation. McNamee's background and actions suggest a willingness to sacrifice environmental and public health protections for the sake of deregulation and fossil fuel promotion, making his policies and intentions deeply alarming and untrustworthy. His vision poses significant risks to the long-term sustainability of U.S. energy policy and the health of our planet.

Section 3:
The General Welfare
13 Environmental Protection Agency
by Mandy M. Gunasekara

- A Cautionary Tale

Gather around, because the events you are about to hear about will make the hairs on your arm stand up. "The General Welfare: Environmental Protection Agency" by Mandy M. Gunasekara is a deeply unsettling blueprint for transforming the mission and operations of the Environmental Protection Agency (EPA). Gunasekara, a former EPA Chief of Staff and a senior policy advisor, outlines a vision that prioritizes deregulation, industry collaboration, and economic growth over environmental protection and public health. Her proposals reflect a drive to shift the EPA's focus towards facilitating industrial interests, raising significant concerns about the erosion of crucial environmental safeguards.

Gunasekara begins by advocating for a substantial rollback of environmental regulations that she argues stifle economic growth and innovation. Gunasekara's aggressive deregulation agenda threatens to dismantle essential protections that safeguard air and water quality, and overall public health. This approach risks increasing pollution and environmental degradation, compromising the well-being of communities across the nation.

A core component of Gunasekara's strategy involves increasing collaboration between the EPA and industry stakeholders. She suggests that close partnerships with industry can lead to more practical and economically viable environmental policies. However, this focus on industry collaboration raises serious concerns about conflicts of interest and the potential for regulatory capture. It risks prioritizing corporate profits over the agency's mission to protect human health and the environment, undermining the integrity and impartiality of the EPA's regulatory processes.

Gunasekara also calls for shifting the EPA's priorities towards economic growth and job creation. She argues that environmental policies should support economic development and not hinder it. This perspective neglects the long-term economic benefits of environmental protection, such as reducing healthcare costs and preserving natural resources. By emphasizing short-term economic gains, Gunasekara's vision overlooks the importance of sustainable development and the need to balance economic growth with environmental stewardship.

In her critique of current EPA policies, Gunasekara emphasizes the need for a more flexible and adaptive regulatory approach. She advocates for streamlining permitting processes and allowing greater regulatory discretion at the state level. This approach risks creating a patchwork of regulations that vary widely in stringency and effectiveness. It could lead to weaker environmental protections in states with fewer resources or less stringent environmental priorities.

Another troubling aspect of Gunasekara's vision is her stance on climate change. She has been known to downplay the urgency of addressing climate change, arguing against stringent regulations aimed at reducing greenhouse gas emissions. This perspective is alarming, given the overwhelming scientific consensus on the need for immediate and decisive action to mitigate climate change impacts. Gunasekara's approach risks stalling progress on critical climate initiatives, exacerbating the global climate crisis.

Gunasekara suggests that voluntary compliance programs and incentives for businesses can be more effective than strict enforcement measures. However, this approach risks reducing accountability for environmental violations and allowing polluters to operate with impunity. Strong enforcement is essential for ensuring compliance and protecting public health and the environment.

In summary, "The General Welfare: Environmental Protection Agency" by Mandy M. Gunasekara presents a vision for the EPA that prioritizes deregulation, industry collaboration, and economic growth. Her proposals for rolling back 74regulations, increasing industry partnerships, and downplaying climate action reflect a troubling shift towards serving corporate interests over environmental protection. This document serves as a foreshadowing of the potential dangers of prioritizing short-term economic gains over long-term environmental stewardship, underscoring the need to preserve a balanced and forward-thinking approach to environmental policy.

Why We Can't Trust Mandy M. Gunasekara

We cannot trust Mandy M. Gunasekara because her background and actions reveal a consistent pattern of prioritizing deregulation and industry interests over environmental protection and public health. As a former EPA Chief of Staff and senior policy advisor, Gunasekara has been a vocal advocate for rolling back environmental regulations, arguing that they stifle economic growth and innovation. Her tenure at the EPA was marked by efforts to reduce regulatory burdens on businesses, reflecting a governance style that values corporate profits over the agency's mission to protect human health and the environment.

One notable example of Gunasekara's controversial approach is her support for dismantling critical environmental regulations that safeguard air and water quality. She has argued that these regulations impose unnecessary burdens on businesses, but this perspective fails to recognize the essential role they play in protecting public health. Gunasekara's push for aggressive deregulation risks increasing pollution and environmental degradation, compromising the well-being of communities across the nation. Her actions suggest a willingness to sacrifice long-term environmental sustainability for short-term economic gains, making her policies deeply alarming.

Moreover, Gunasekara's stance on climate change further highlights her problematic approach. She has been known to downplay the urgency of addressing climate change, arguing against stringent regulations aimed at reducing greenhouse gas emissions. This perspective is alarming given the overwhelming scientific consensus on the need for immediate and decisive action to mitigate climate change impacts. Gunasekara's background and actions suggest a disregard for the critical importance of climate action, posing significant risks to global efforts to combat climate change. Her vision for the EPA prioritizes industry collaboration and economic growth over the agency's core mission, making her policies and intentions untrustworthy. Her approach threatens to undermine crucial environmental protections and stall progress on critical climate initiatives.

Section 3:
The General Welfare
14 Department of Health and Human Services
by Roger Severino

- A Cautionary Tale

Folks, prepare yourselves for what is about to be revealed; it's nothing short of terrifying. "The General Welfare: Department of Health & Human Services" by Roger Severino is a profoundly unsettling blueprint for transforming America's health and human services landscape. Severino, a former Director of the Office for Civil Rights at HHS, outlines a vision that prioritizes deregulation, religious liberty, and conservative values over comprehensive healthcare access and public health protections. His proposals reflect a drive to reshape HHS into an entity that aligns with conservative ideological goals, raising significant concerns about the erosion of healthcare equity and the protection of vulnerable populations.

Severino begins by advocating for significant deregulation of the healthcare sector. He argues that reducing regulatory burdens will spur innovation and reduce costs. Severino's approach threatens to undermine protections that ensure patient safety and equitable access to care. His focus on deregulation risks compromising the quality of healthcare services and could exacerbate existing disparities, particularly for low-income and marginalized communities.

A core component of Severino's strategy involves promoting religious liberty within the healthcare system. He suggests that healthcare providers should have the right to refuse services based on their religious beliefs. While protecting religious freedom is important, this approach could lead to widespread discrimination and denial of essential health services to vulnerable groups, including LGBTQ+ individuals and women seeking reproductive healthcare. Severino's emphasis on religious liberty over patient rights raises serious ethical concerns about the balance between individual beliefs and public health needs.

Severino also calls for reducing federal oversight and increasing state control over health and human services programs. He argues that states are better equipped to manage these programs without federal interference. States with fewer resources may struggle to provide comprehensive care, leading to significant inequalities in health outcomes across the country.

In his critique of current HHS policies, Severino emphasizes the need for a market-driven approach to healthcare. He advocates for reducing government intervention and allowing market forces to dictate the availability and cost of health services. This laissez-faire philosophy ignores the unique challenges of the healthcare sector, where market dynamics often fail to address the needs of the most vulnerable. Without adequate government intervention, many individuals could be left without access to necessary care, exacerbating health inequities.

Another troubling aspect of Severino's vision is his stance on public health funding. He proposes significant cuts to programs aimed at addressing public health crises, such as infectious disease outbreaks and chronic illnesses. Severino argues that these programs are inefficient and costly. However, reducing funding for public health initiatives could leave the nation unprepared to respond to health emergencies, putting countless lives at risk.

Severino's proposals also include limiting the scope of federal health programs like Medicaid and Medicare. He argues that these programs create dependency and should be restructured to encourage personal responsibility. However, cutting these programs would disproportionately affect low-income individuals, seniors, and people with disabilities, increasing health disparities and undermining the safety net that millions of Americans rely on.

In summary, "The General Welfare: Department of Health & Human Services" by Roger Severino presents a vision for U.S. health policy that prioritizes deregulation, religious liberty, and state control. His proposals for reducing federal oversight, promoting market-driven healthcare, and cutting public health funding reflect a troubling shift towards serving conservative ideological goals over the needs of all Americans. This document serves as a caution of the potential dangers of prioritizing ideological conformity over the fundamental goals of public health and human services, underscoring the need to preserve a balanced and compassionate approach to health policy.

Why We Can't Trust Roger Severino

We cannot trust Roger Severino because his background and actions reveal a consistent pattern of prioritizing conservative ideological goals over comprehensive healthcare access and public health protections. As a former Director of the Office for Civil Rights at the Department of Health and Human Services (HHS), Severino has been a vocal advocate for policies that promote religious liberty at the expense of patient rights and healthcare equity. His tenure was marked by efforts to allow healthcare providers to refuse services based on religious beliefs, reflecting a governance style that values ideological conformity over the health and well-being of all individuals.

One notable example of Severino's controversial approach is his support for expanding religious exemptions within healthcare. He argued that healthcare providers should have the right to refuse services such as contraception and gender-affirming care if they conflict with their religious beliefs. While religious freedom is important, this stance can lead to widespread discrimination and denial of essential health services to vulnerable populations, including LGBTQ+ individuals and women seeking reproductive healthcare. Severino's policies risk creating significant barriers to care for those who need it most, exacerbating health disparities.

Moreover, Severino's stance on reducing federal oversight in favor of state control further highlights his problematic approach. He advocated for increased state control over health and human services programs, arguing that states are better equipped to manage these programs. However, this strategy risks creating a fragmented healthcare system with varying levels of quality and accessibility. Severino's background and actions suggest a willingness to sacrifice the consistency and equity provided by federal oversight for the sake of ideological goals.

In summary, Roger Severino's background and policies prioritize conservative values over equitable healthcare access and public health protections. His advocacy for religious exemptions and reduced federal oversight poses significant risks to vulnerable populations and undermines the principles of equity and access in healthcare.

Section 3:
The General Welfare
15 Department of Housing and Urban Development
by Ben Carson

- A Cautionary Tale

Everyone, brace yourselves for the unsettling story you are about to hear. "The General Welfare: Department of Housing and Urban Development" by Ben Carson is a profoundly unsettling blueprint for transforming America's housing policies. Carson, a former Secretary of Housing and Urban Development (HUD), outlines a vision that prioritizes deregulation, market-driven solutions, and reduced federal intervention over affordable housing and support for vulnerable populations. His proposals reflect a drive to reshape HUD into an entity that aligns with conservative ideological goals, raising significant concerns about the erosion of housing equity and the protection of those in need.

Carson begins by advocating for significant deregulation of the housing market. He argues that reducing regulatory burdens will spur development and lower housing costs. While streamlining some regulations can be beneficial, Carson's approach threatens to undermine essential protections that ensure safe and affordable housing. His focus on deregulation risks increasing housing instability and compromising the quality of housing, particularly for low-income families and marginalized communities.

A core component of Carson's strategy involves promoting public-private partnerships to address housing issues. He suggests that collaboration with private developers can lead to innovative and cost-effective solutions. However, this approach often prioritizes profit over people. Without strict oversight, these partnerships can lead to the displacement of low-income residents and the creation of housing that is unaffordable for those most in need. Carson's emphasis on market-driven solutions overlooks the complex social dynamics that contribute to housing inequality.

Carson also calls for reducing federal oversight and increasing state and local control over housing policies. He argues that local governments are better equipped to manage housing issues without federal interference. While local control can lead to more tailored solutions, this approach risks creating a patchwork of housing policies with varying levels of effectiveness. States and localities with fewer resources may struggle to address housing needs, leading to significant disparities in housing quality and access across the country.

In his critique of current HUD policies, Carson emphasizes the need for personal responsibility and self-sufficiency. He advocates for programs that encourage individuals to move towards homeownership and reduce dependence on government assistance. While promoting self-sufficiency is important, Carson's approach fails to recognize the structural barriers that many individuals face in achieving stable housing. His policies risk leaving behind those who are most vulnerable, including the homeless, disabled, and elderly.

Another troubling aspect of Carson's vision is his stance on affordable housing programs. He proposes cutting funding for programs such as Section 8 vouchers, which provide critical support to low-income families. Carson argues that these programs create dependency and are inefficient. However, reducing funding for affordable housing initiatives would disproportionately affect the most disadvantaged populations, increasing housing insecurity and homelessness.

Carson's proposals also include rolling back fair housing regulations that protect against discrimination. He suggests that these regulations are overly burdensome for developers and hinder economic growth. This perspective ignores the persistent issues of housing discrimination and segregation that these regulations aim to address. Weakening fair housing protections could lead to increased discrimination and reduced access to housing for minority communities.

In summary, "The General Welfare: Department of Housing and Urban Development" by Ben Carson presents a vision for U.S. housing policy that prioritizes deregulation, market-driven solutions, and reduced federal oversight. His proposals for promoting public-private partnerships, cutting funding for affordable housing programs, and rolling back fair housing regulations reflect a troubling shift towards serving conservative ideological goals over the needs of vulnerable populations. This document serves as a warning of the potential dangers of prioritizing market solutions over the fundamental goals of housing security and social justice.

Why We Can't Trust Ben Carson

We cannot trust Ben Carson because his background and actions reveal a consistent pattern of prioritizing market-driven solutions and deregulation over the fundamental needs of vulnerable populations. As the former Secretary of Housing and Urban Development (HUD), Carson has been a vocal advocate for reducing federal oversight and promoting public-private partnerships. His tenure at HUD was marked by efforts to roll back regulations and cut funding for critical housing programs, reflecting a governance style that values market efficiency over housing equity and security.

One notable example of Carson's controversial approach is his support for significant deregulation of the housing market. He argued that reducing regulatory burdens would spur development and lower housing costs. However, this perspective fails to recognize the essential role of regulations in ensuring safe and affordable housing. Carson's push for deregulation risks increasing housing instability and compromising the quality of housing, particularly for low-income families and marginalized communities.

Moreover, Carson's stance on reducing federal oversight in favor of state and local control further underscores his problematic approach. He advocated for increasing state and local control over housing policies, arguing that local governments are better equipped to manage these issues. However, this strategy risks creating a fragmented housing system with varying levels of effectiveness. States with fewer resources may struggle to address housing needs, leading to significant disparities in housing quality and access across the country. Carson's background and actions suggest a preference for a decentralized approach that often leaves the most vulnerable populations without adequate support.

In summary, Ben Carson's background and policies prioritize market-driven solutions and deregulation over the needs of vulnerable populations. His advocacy for reducing federal oversight and cutting funding for critical housing programs poses significant risks to housing equity and security. Carson's approach undermines the principles of equity and access in housing policy, making his policies and intentions deeply incredulous and untrustworthy.

Section 3:
The General Welfare
16 Department of the Interior
by William Perry Pendley

- A Cautionary Tale

Gather around, because the events you are about to hear about are truly disturbing. "The General Welfare: Department of the Interior" by William Perry Pendley is a deeply troubling manifesto for reshaping America's management of its natural resources and public lands. Pendley, a former acting director of the Bureau of Land Management, outlines a vision that prioritizes deregulation, resource extraction, and reduced federal oversight over conservation and environmental protection. His proposals reflect a drive to transform the Department of the Interior into an entity that aligns with corporate interests, raising significant concerns about the preservation of public lands and natural resources.

Pendley begins by advocating for a significant rollback of regulations that he argues hinder economic growth and resource development. He claims that these regulations impose unnecessary burdens on industries such as mining, logging, and oil and gas extraction. While reducing some regulatory burdens can promote economic activity, Pendley's approach threatens to dismantle essential protections that safeguard the environment and public health. This aggressive deregulation risks increasing pollution, habitat destruction, and the exploitation of natural resources without regard for sustainability.

A core component of Pendley's strategy involves increasing access to public lands for resource extraction. He argues that opening more federal lands to industry will create jobs and boost the economy. However, this perspective overlooks the long-term environmental costs of such activities. Pendley's vision prioritizes short-term economic gains over the preservation of ecosystems and biodiversity. By promoting extensive resource extraction, his policies could lead to irreversible damage to some of the nation's most cherished natural landscapes.

Pendley also calls for reducing federal oversight and transferring more control over public lands to state and local governments. He asserts that local authorities are better equipped to manage these lands effectively. While local control can offer tailored solutions, this approach risks creating a fragmented system with inconsistent protections. States with fewer resources or differing priorities may struggle to implement effective conservation measures, leading to significant disparities in the management and preservation of public lands across the country.

In his critique of current Interior Department policies, Pendley emphasizes the need for a market-driven approach to land management. He advocates for reducing the role of government and allowing market forces to dictate the use of natural resources. This laissez-faire philosophy ignores the unique challenges of land and resource management, where market dynamics often fail to account for environmental externalities. Without adequate regulation and oversight, resource extraction activities could prioritize profits over environmental sustainability and public welfare.

Another troubling aspect of Pendley's vision is his stance on environmental conservation programs. He proposes cutting funding for initiatives aimed at protecting endangered species and preserving natural habitats. Pendley argues that these programs are costly and inefficient. However, reducing support for conservation efforts would jeopardize biodiversity and undermine efforts to protect vulnerable species from extinction. His approach threatens to reverse decades of progress in environmental conservation.

In summary, "The General Welfare: Department of the Interior" by William Perry Pendley presents a vision for U.S. land and resource management that prioritizes deregulation, resource extraction, and reduced federal oversight. His proposals for rolling back regulations, increasing access to public lands for industry, and cutting funding for conservation programs reflect a troubling shift towards serving corporate interests over environmental protection. Pendley's vision neglects the broader principles of sustainability and conservation. This document serves as a window into the dangers of prioritizing economic gains over the long-term health of the nation's natural resources, underscoring the need to preserve a balanced and forward-thinking approach to land management.

Why We Can't Trust William Perry Pendley

We cannot trust William Perry Pendley because his background and actions reveal a consistent pattern of prioritizing deregulation and resource extraction over environmental protection and conservation. As the former acting director of the Bureau of Land Management (BLM), Pendley has been a vocal advocate for opening public lands to extensive industrial activities such as mining, logging, and oil and gas drilling. His tenure at BLM was marked by efforts to reduce regulatory oversight and promote the interests of extractive industries, reflecting a governance style that values economic exploitation over the preservation of natural resources.

One notable example of Pendley's controversial approach is his push to open vast tracts of federal land to resource extraction. He argued that this would create jobs and boost the economy, but this perspective fails to account for the long-term environmental damage caused by such activities. Pendley's policies risk significant habitat destruction, increased pollution, and the depletion of natural resources, prioritizing short-term economic gains over sustainable land management.

Moreover, Pendley's stance on reducing federal oversight and transferring control of public lands to state and local governments further underscores his problematic approach. He advocated for local control, arguing that states are better equipped to manage these lands. However, this strategy risks creating a fragmented system with inconsistent protections. States with fewer resources or differing priorities may struggle to implement effective conservation measures, leading to significant disparities in the management and preservation of public lands across the country.

In summary, William Perry Pendley's background and policies prioritize deregulation and resource extraction over environmental protection and conservation. His advocacy for opening public lands to industrial activities and reducing federal oversight poses significant risks to the health of the nation's natural resources. Pendley's approach undermines the principles of sustainable land management, making his policies and intentions deeply unmanageable and untrustworthy.

Section 3:
The General Welfare
17 Department of Justice
by Gene Hamilton

- A Cautionary Tale

Friends, hold on tight; the tale you are about to hear is absolutely bone-chilling. "The General Welfare: Department of Justice" by Gene Hamilton is a deeply troubling manifesto for transforming the Department of Justice (DOJ). Hamilton, a former senior official in the Trump administration, outlines a vision that prioritizes aggressive law enforcement, deregulation, and conservative values over civil rights and social justice. His proposals will reshape the DOJ into an entity that aligns with a conservative ideological agenda, raising significant concerns about the erosion of legal protections for vulnerable populations and the potential for increased governmental overreach.

Hamilton begins by advocating for a significant increase in law enforcement resources. He argues that bolstering police forces and federal law enforcement agencies is essential for maintaining public order and safety. While ensuring public safety is crucial, Hamilton's emphasis on aggressive law enforcement raises concerns about potential abuses of power and the erosion of civil liberties. His approach risks exacerbating tensions between law enforcement and communities, particularly those of color, which have historically faced disproportionate policing.

A core component of Hamilton's strategy involves rolling back regulations that he claims hinder law enforcement effectiveness. He proposes reducing oversight and accountability measures that have been put in place to prevent abuse and ensure justice. Deregulating law enforcement can lead to unchecked power and a lack of transparency, undermining public trust in the justice system. Hamilton's vision prioritizes efficiency over accountability, threatening to weaken the safeguards that protect individuals from government overreach.

Hamilton also calls for a more stringent approach to immigration enforcement. He argues for increased resources and authority for Immigration and Customs Enforcement (ICE) and stricter immigration policies. This focus on aggressive immigration enforcement risks criminalizing immigrant communities and perpetuating a climate of fear and discrimination. Hamilton's policies could lead to widespread detentions and deportations, often without due process, violating the rights of immigrants and their families.

In his critique of current DOJ policies, Hamilton emphasizes the need for a more conservative approach to civil rights. He suggests that recent advances in civil rights protections have gone too far and need to be curtailed. This perspective undermines the progress made in promoting equality and justice for marginalized groups, including LGBTQ+ individuals, people of color, and women. Hamilton's vision threatens to roll back critical protections and reinforce systemic inequalities.

Another troubling aspect of Hamilton's vision is his stance on judicial appointments. He advocates for appointing judges who adhere strictly to conservative interpretations of the Constitution. While appointing qualified judges is important, Hamilton's approach risks politicizing the judiciary and undermining its independence. This focus on ideological purity over judicial impartiality threatens to erode the foundational principle of an independent judiciary.

Hamilton's proposals also include reducing federal oversight of state and local law enforcement agencies. However, this approach risks creating a patchwork of justice systems with varying levels of accountability and effectiveness. States with fewer resources may struggle to implement effective oversight, leading to disparities in the administration of justice.

In summary, "The General Welfare: Department of Justice" by Gene Hamilton presents a vision for the DOJ that prioritizes aggressive law enforcement, deregulation, and conservative values. His proposals for increasing law enforcement resources, rolling back regulations, and adopting a stringent approach to immigration enforcement reflect a troubling shift towards serving conservative ideological goals over the needs of all Americans. This document serves as a crude reminder of the potential dangers of prioritizing ideological conformity over the fundamental goals of justice and equality, underscoring the need to preserve a balanced and fair approach to justice policy.

Why We Can't Trust Gene Hamilton

We cannot trust Gene Hamilton because his background and actions reveal a consistent pattern of prioritizing conservative ideological goals over civil rights and social justice. As a former senior official in the Trump administration, Hamilton played a significant role in shaping policies that aggressively targeted immigrant communities and sought to curtail civil rights protections. His tenure was marked by efforts to expand the authority of Immigration and Customs Enforcement (ICE) and implement stricter immigration policies, often at the expense of due process and human rights. This approach reflects a governance style that values enforcement and control over compassion and justice.

One notable example of Hamilton's controversial approach is his advocacy for rolling back regulations designed to ensure accountability and prevent abuse within law enforcement. He has argued for reducing oversight of police and federal law enforcement agencies, claiming that such measures hinder their effectiveness. However, this perspective fails to recognize the importance of transparency and accountability in maintaining public trust. Hamilton's push for deregulation risks enabling unchecked power and abuse, exacerbating tensions between law enforcement and communities, particularly those of color who have historically faced disproportionate policing.

Moreover, Hamilton's stance on judicial appointments further highlights his problematic approach. He has consistently advocated for appointing judges who adhere strictly to conservative interpretations of the Constitution, prioritizing ideological purity over judicial impartiality. This focus on politicizing the judiciary threatens to undermine its independence, a cornerstone of a fair and balanced justice system. Hamilton's background and actions suggest a willingness to sacrifice the principles of justice and equality for the sake of advancing a conservative agenda, making his policies and intentions deeply undemocratic and untrustworthy. His vision for the Department of Justice poses significant risks to the foundational principles of civil rights and social justice.

Section 3:
The General Welfare
18 Department of Labor & Related Agencies
by Jonathon Berry

- A Cautionary Tale

Attention, all, for the story you are about to hear is more horrifying than you can imagine. "The General Welfare: Department of Labor and Related Agencies" by Jonathon Berry is a deeply troubling blueprint for transforming America's labor policies. Berry, a former senior official in the Trump administration, outlines a vision that prioritizes deregulation, reduced union influence, and a market-driven approach over worker protections and labor rights. His proposals reflect a drive to reshape the Department of Labor (DOL) into an entity that aligns with corporate interests, raising significant concerns about the erosion of labor rights and the well-being of American workers.

Berry begins by advocating for significant deregulation of labor laws. He argues that reducing regulatory burdens will spur economic growth and create jobs. While streamlining some regulations can promote business efficiency, Berry's approach threatens to undermine essential protections for workers. His focus on deregulation risks increasing workplace hazards, lowering wages, and reducing job security, particularly for low-income and vulnerable workers. This aggressive deregulation could lead to a race to the bottom, where labor standards are sacrificed for profits.

A core component of Berry's strategy involves weakening the influence of labor unions. He suggests that unions have too much power and that reducing their influence will lead to a more flexible and competitive labor market. However, this perspective fails to recognize the crucial role unions play in advocating for fair wages, safe working conditions, and benefits for workers. Berry's vision could lead to diminished collective bargaining power and a deterioration of workers' rights and benefits. Without strong unions, workers may find it harder to stand up against exploitative practices.

Berry also calls for reducing federal oversight of labor practices and shifting more control to states and local governments. He argues that local control allows for more tailored and effective labor policies. While decentralization can lead to more customized solutions, this approach risks creating a fragmented system with varying levels of worker protections. States with fewer resources or differing priorities may struggle to enforce labor laws effectively, leading to significant disparities in workers' rights across the country. This patchwork approach could result in uneven protections and greater inequality.

In his critique of current labor policies, Berry emphasizes the need for a market-driven approach to employment. He advocates for reducing the role of government and allowing market forces to dictate employment practices. This laissez-faire philosophy overlooks the unique challenges of the labor market, where power imbalances between employers and employees can lead to exploitation. Without adequate regulation and oversight, workers may face increased exploitation and abuse. The market alone cannot be trusted to protect workers' interests.

Another troubling aspect of Berry's vision is his stance on labor standards and wage protections. He proposes rolling back minimum wage laws and other labor standards that he argues are burdensome for businesses. This perspective ignores the importance of these standards in ensuring a livable wage and fair working conditions for all workers. Berry's approach risks widening the gap between the rich and the poor and increasing economic inequality. By reducing wage protections, he undermines the foundation of economic justice.

In summary, "The General Welfare: Department of Labor and Related Agencies" by Jonathon Berry presents a vision for U.S. labor policy that prioritizes deregulation, reduced union influence, and a market-driven approach. His proposals for rolling back labor regulations, weakening union power, and reducing federal oversight reflect a troubling shift towards serving corporate interests over the needs of workers. Berry's vision neglects the broader principles of labor rights, economic equality, and worker protections. This document serves as a threat of the potential dangers of prioritizing market efficiency over the fundamental goals of labor justice and social welfare, underscoring the need to preserve a balanced and fair approach to labor policy.

Why We Can't Trust Jonathon Berry

We cannot trust Jonathon Berry because his background and actions reveal a consistent pattern of prioritizing corporate interests and deregulation over the fundamental rights and protections of workers. As a former senior official in the Trump administration, Berry has been a vocal advocate for reducing labor regulations and weakening the influence of unions. His tenure was marked by efforts to roll back essential worker protections, reflecting a governance style that values market efficiency and corporate profits over the well-being of American workers.

One notable example of Berry's controversial approach is his push to deregulate labor laws, arguing that reducing regulatory burdens will spur economic growth and job creation. However, this perspective fails to acknowledge the critical role of regulations in ensuring safe working conditions, fair wages, and job security. By advocating for extensive deregulation, Berry risks increasing workplace hazards and exploitation, particularly for low-income and vulnerable workers who depend on these protections. His actions suggest a willingness to sacrifice worker safety and security for short-term economic gains.

Moreover, Berry's stance on reducing the influence of labor unions further underscores his problematic approach. He has consistently argued that unions hold too much power and that diminishing their influence will lead to a more competitive labor market. This view ignores the vital role unions play in advocating for workers' rights, including fair wages, benefits, and safe working conditions.

By weakening unions, Berry's policies could lead to diminished collective bargaining power, leaving workers with less ability to negotiate for better conditions and protections. His background and actions indicate a preference for empowering employers at the expense of employees, making his policies and intentions deeply biased against labor and untrustworthy. Berry's vision for labor policy threatens to widen economic inequality and undermine the hard-won rights and protections that workers rely on.

Section 3:
The General Welfare
19 Department of Transportation
by Diana Furchtgott-Roth

- A Cautionary Tale

Come closer, everyone, because what you are about to learn is
terrifying beyond belief. "The General Welfare: Department of
Transportation" by Diana Furchtgott-Roth is a profoundly unsettling
blueprint for transforming America's transportation policies.
Furchtgott-Roth, a former Deputy Assistant Secretary for Research
and Technology at the Department of Transportation, outlines a
vision that prioritizes deregulation, privatization, and market-driven
solutions over public safety and equitable access to transportation.
Her proposals reflect a drive to reshape the Department of
Transportation (DOT) into an entity that aligns with corporate
interests, raising significant concerns about the erosion of safety
standards and the neglect of underserved communities.

Furchtgott-Roth begins by advocating for significant deregulation of
transportation industries. She argues that reducing regulatory burdens
will spur innovation and economic growth. While streamlining some
regulations can indeed promote efficiency, Furchtgott-Roth's
approach threatens to undermine essential safety standards. Her focus
on deregulation risks increasing the likelihood of accidents and
compromising the integrity of transportation infrastructure,
particularly in critical areas like aviation, rail, and highways.

A core component of Furchtgott-Roth's strategy involves promoting
the privatization of public transportation services. She suggests that
private companies can provide these services more efficiently than the
government. However, this perspective fails to recognize the essential
role of public transportation in ensuring equitable access to mobility.
Privatization could lead to higher costs and reduced service quality for
low-income and rural communities, exacerbating social and economic
disparities.

Furchtgott-Roth also calls for reducing federal oversight of
transportation projects and shifting more control to states and local
governments. She argues that local control allows for more tailored

and effective transportation solutions. While local governance can lead to customized approaches, this strategy risks creating a fragmented system with inconsistent safety and quality standards. States with fewer resources or differing priorities may struggle to maintain robust transportation networks, leading to significant disparities across the country.

In her critique of current DOT policies, Furchtgott-Roth emphasizes the need for a market-driven approach to transportation. She advocates for reducing the role of government and allowing market forces to dictate transportation development and maintenance. This laissez-faire philosophy overlooks the unique challenges of the transportation sector, where public investment and oversight are crucial for ensuring safety, accessibility, and long-term sustainability. Without adequate regulation, transportation infrastructure could deteriorate, and safety standards could be compromised.

Another troubling aspect of Furchtgott-Roth's vision is her stance on environmental regulations related to transportation. She proposes rolling back regulations aimed at reducing emissions and promoting sustainable transportation alternatives. This perspective ignores the urgent need to address climate change and the role of transportation in contributing to greenhouse gas emissions. Furchtgott-Roth's approach risks undermining efforts to transition to cleaner, more sustainable transportation options, jeopardizing environmental and public health.

In summary, "The General Welfare: Department of Transportation" by Diana Furchtgott-Roth presents a vision for U.S. transportation policy that prioritizes deregulation, privatization, and market-driven solutions. Her proposals for rolling back safety regulations, promoting privatization, and reducing federal oversight reflect a troubling shift towards serving corporate interests over public welfare. Furchtgott-Roth's vision neglects the broader principles of safety, accessibility, and sustainability. This document serves as a reminder of the potential dangers of prioritizing market efficiency over the fundamental goals of public transportation and infrastructure, underscoring the need to preserve a balanced and fair approach to transportation policy.

Why We Can't Trust Diana Furchtgott-Roth

We cannot trust Diana Furchtgott-Roth because her background and actions reveal a consistent pattern of prioritizing deregulation and privatization over public safety and equitable access to transportation. As a former Deputy Assistant Secretary for Research and Technology at the Department of Transportation, Furchtgott-Roth has been a vocal advocate for reducing regulatory burdens on transportation industries, arguing that it will spur innovation and economic growth. However, this perspective fails to recognize the critical role of regulations in ensuring safety and maintaining the integrity of transportation infrastructure. Her push for deregulation risks increasing the likelihood of accidents and compromising public safety.

One notable example of Furchtgott-Roth's controversial approach is her advocacy for the privatization of public transportation services. She argues that private companies can provide these services more efficiently than the government. However, this stance overlooks the essential role of public transportation in ensuring equitable access to mobility for all citizens. Privatization could lead to higher costs and reduced service quality for low-income and rural communities, exacerbating social and economic disparities. Furchtgott-Roth's focus on market-driven solutions neglects the needs of underserved populations and threatens to deepen existing inequalities.

Moreover, Furchtgott-Roth's stance on environmental regulations related to transportation further highlights her problematic approach. She has proposed rolling back regulations aimed at reducing emissions and promoting sustainable transportation alternatives. This perspective ignores the urgent need to address climate change and the significant role of the transportation sector in contributing to greenhouse gas emissions.

By undermining efforts to transition to cleaner, more sustainable transportation options, Furchtgott-Roth's policies risk jeopardizing environmental and public health. Her background and actions suggest a governance style that values economic efficiency and corporate interests over the well-being of the public and the environment, making her policies and intentions deeply disturbing and untrustworthy.

Section 3:
The General Welfare
20 Department of Veterans Affairs
by Brooks D. Tucker

- A Cautionary Tale

Listen up, folks, because the events you are about to learn about are terrifying beyond belief. "The General Welfare: Department of Veterans Affairs" by Brooks D. Tucker is a deeply unsettling blueprint for reshaping the policies and operations of the Department of Veterans Affairs (VA). Tucker, a former Assistant Secretary for VA, outlines a vision that prioritizes privatization, deregulation, and market-driven solutions over comprehensive care and support for veterans. His proposals reflect a drive to transform the VA into an entity that aligns with corporate interests, raising significant concerns about the erosion of quality care and services for veterans.

Tucker begins by advocating for the significant privatization of VA services. He argues that private healthcare providers can deliver services more efficiently and effectively than the VA. While partnerships with private providers can sometimes enhance service delivery, Tucker's approach risks fragmenting veterans' healthcare and reducing the quality of care. Privatization could lead to inconsistencies in care standards and access, especially for veterans in rural or underserved areas.

A core component of Tucker's strategy involves reducing federal oversight and regulations within the VA. He claims that deregulation will streamline operations and cut costs. However, this perspective overlooks the importance of regulations in ensuring the safety and quality of care provided to veterans. Reducing oversight could lead to lapses in care, increased errors, and compromised patient safety.

Tucker also emphasizes the need for a market-driven approach to veteran services. He advocates for reducing the role of the government and allowing market forces to dictate service provision. This laissez-faire philosophy ignores the unique needs of veterans, who often require specialized care and support that the private market may not adequately provide. Without robust government involvement, many veterans could be left without the necessary care and services.

In his critique of current VA policies, Tucker highlights the inefficiencies and bureaucratic hurdles within the department. He proposes cutting back on administrative processes to enhance efficiency. While reducing unnecessary bureaucracy is essential, Tucker's approach risks eliminating critical oversight mechanisms that ensure accountability and quality within the VA. Streamlining processes should not come at the expense of the safeguards that protect veterans' interests.

Another troubling aspect of Tucker's vision is his stance on the VA's role in providing mental health services. He suggests that private mental health providers can meet veterans' needs more effectively. However, mental health care for veterans often requires a deep understanding of military culture and the specific challenges faced by veterans. Privatizing these services risks creating gaps in care and reducing the effectiveness of mental health support.

Tucker's proposals also include reducing funding for various veteran support programs, arguing that these programs create dependency and are financially unsustainable. However, cutting these programs would disproportionately affect veterans who rely on them for essential services, such as housing assistance and job training. These cuts could lead to increased homelessness and unemployment among veterans, exacerbating the very issues the VA is meant to address.

In summary, "The General Welfare: Department of Veterans Affairs" by Brooks D. Tucker presents a vision for the VA that prioritizes privatization, deregulation, and market-driven solutions. His proposals for reducing federal oversight, promoting privatization, and cutting funding for veteran support programs reflect a troubling shift towards serving corporate interests over the needs of veterans. Tucker's vision neglects the broader principles of comprehensive care and support that veterans deserve. This document serves as a pointed reminder of the potential dangers of prioritizing market efficiency over the fundamental goals of veteran welfare, underscoring the need to preserve a balanced and compassionate approach to VA policy.

Why We Can't Trust Brooks D. Tucker

We cannot trust Brooks D. Tucker because his background and actions reveal a consistent pattern of prioritizing privatization and market-driven solutions over the comprehensive care and support that veterans desperately need. As a former Assistant Secretary for the Department of Veterans Affairs (VA), Tucker has been a vocal advocate for reducing the role of government in providing veteran services, arguing that private healthcare providers can deliver better and more efficient care. This perspective fails to recognize the unique needs of veterans, many of whom require specialized care that private providers may not adequately address. His push for privatization risks fragmenting veterans' healthcare, leading to inconsistencies in care standards and access, particularly for those in rural or underserved areas.

One notable example of Tucker's controversial approach is his emphasis on reducing federal oversight and regulations within the VA. He has argued that deregulation will streamline operations and cut costs, but this viewpoint overlooks the critical role of regulations in ensuring the safety and quality of care provided to veterans. During his tenure, efforts to deregulate the VA could have led to lapses in care, increased errors, and compromised patient safety. Tucker's focus on cutting bureaucratic processes risks eliminating essential oversight mechanisms that protect veterans' interests, making his policies deeply unpatriotic and upsetting.

Moreover, Tucker's stance on funding reductions for various veteran support programs further highlights his problematic approach. He has suggested that these programs create dependency and are financially unsustainable, advocating for significant cuts. However, reducing funding for essential services like housing assistance and job training would disproportionately affect veterans who rely on them. These cuts could lead to increased homelessness and unemployment among veterans, exacerbating the very issues the VA is meant to address. Tucker's background and actions indicate a preference for market efficiency over the well-being of veterans, making his policies and intentions untrustworthy. His vision for the VA undermines the comprehensive care and support that veterans deserve, posing significant risks to their welfare.

Section 4:
The Economy
21 Department of Commerce
by Thomas F. Gilman

- A Cautionary Tale

Gather around, for the story you are about to hear is nothing short of a nightmare. "The Economy: Department of Commerce" by Thomas F. Gilman is a profoundly unsettling blueprint for transforming America's economic policies. Gilman, a former senior official in the Department of Commerce, outlines a vision that prioritizes deregulation, privatization, and market-driven solutions over comprehensive economic oversight and equitable growth. His proposals reflect a drive to reshape the Department of Commerce into an entity that aligns with corporate interests, raising significant concerns about the erosion of economic fairness and the neglect of small businesses and vulnerable communities.

Gilman begins by advocating for significant deregulation of business and trade practices. He argues that reducing regulatory burdens will spur innovation and economic growth. While streamlining some regulations can indeed promote efficiency, Gilman's approach threatens to undermine essential protections for consumers, workers, and the environment. His focus on deregulation risks increasing corporate abuses, reducing workplace safety, and exacerbating environmental degradation.

A core component of Gilman's strategy involves promoting the privatization of various economic functions currently managed by the government. He suggests that private companies can provide these services more efficiently. However, this perspective fails to recognize the essential role of government in ensuring fair competition, protecting public interests, and providing essential services that the private sector may neglect. Privatization could lead to higher costs and reduced service quality, particularly for low-income and marginalized communities.

Gilman also calls for reducing federal oversight of commerce-related activities and shifting more control to states and local governments. He argues that local control allows for more tailored and effective economic policies. While local governance can lead to customized approaches, this strategy risks creating a fragmented system with inconsistent protections. States with fewer resources or differing priorities may struggle to maintain robust economic oversight, leading to significant disparities across the country.

In his critique of current Commerce Department policies, Gilman emphasizes the need for a market-driven approach to economic development. He advocates for reducing the role of government and allowing market forces to dictate economic outcomes. This laissez-faire philosophy overlooks the unique challenges of the economy, where market dynamics often fail to address the needs of the most vulnerable. Without adequate regulation and oversight, economic inequalities can deepen, and public welfare can suffer.

Another troubling aspect of Gilman's vision is his stance on international trade. He proposes rolling back trade regulations and promoting free trade agreements without sufficient safeguards. This perspective ignores the need for balanced trade policies that protect domestic industries and workers from unfair competition and exploitation. Gilman's approach risks undermining American jobs and contributing to the decline of critical industries.

Gilman's proposals also include reducing funding for economic research and development programs. However, cutting public investment in R&D could hinder the development of new technologies and slow economic progress. Public funding is crucial for addressing long-term challenges and fostering broad-based innovation.

In summary, "The Economy: Department of Commerce" by Thomas F. Gilman presents a vision for U.S. economic policy that prioritizes deregulation, privatization, and market-driven solutions. His proposals for rolling back regulations, promoting privatization, and reducing federal oversight reflect a troubling shift towards serving corporate interests over public welfare. Gilman's vision neglects the broader principles of economic fairness, equity, and comprehensive oversight. This document serves as a dire reminder of the potential dangers of prioritizing market efficiency over the fundamental goals of economic justice and social welfare, underscoring the need to preserve a balanced and fair approach to economic policy.

Why We Can't Trust Thomas F. Gilman

We cannot trust Thomas F. Gilman because his background and actions reveal a consistent pattern of prioritizing corporate interests and deregulation over the fundamental principles of economic fairness and public welfare. As a former senior official in the Department of Commerce, Gilman has been a vocal advocate for reducing regulatory burdens on businesses, arguing that this will spur innovation and economic growth. However, this perspective fails to recognize the critical role of regulations in protecting consumers, workers, and the environment. His push for extensive deregulation risks increasing corporate abuses, reducing workplace safety, and exacerbating environmental degradation.

One notable example of Gilman's controversial approach is his support for the privatization of various economic functions currently managed by the government. He argues that private companies can provide these services more efficiently. However, this stance overlooks the essential role of government in ensuring fair competition, protecting public interests, and providing essential services that the private sector may neglect. During his tenure, efforts to promote privatization could have led to higher costs and reduced service quality, particularly for low-income and marginalized communities, exacerbating social and economic disparities.

Moreover, Gilman's stance on international trade further highlights his problematic approach. He has proposed rolling back trade regulations and promoting free trade agreements without sufficient safeguards, arguing that this will benefit the economy. However, this perspective ignores the need for balanced trade policies that protect domestic industries and workers from unfair competition and exploitation. Gilman's background and actions suggest a willingness to sacrifice American jobs and critical industries for the sake of market efficiency. His vision for economic policy undermines the comprehensive oversight and balanced approach necessary to address the complex challenges of a fair and equitable economy, making his policies and intentions deeply disingenuous and untrustworthy.

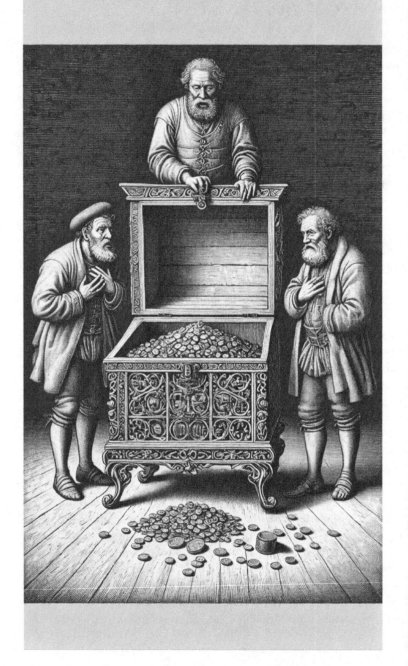

Section 4:
The Economy
22 Department of the Treasury
by William Walton, Stephan Moore, and David R. Burton

- A Cautionary Tale

Alright, everyone, get ready, because what you are about to learn will haunt you for eternity. "The Economy: Department of the Treasury" by William Walton, Stephen Moore, and David R. Burton is a profoundly unsettling blueprint for transforming America's fiscal policies. Walton, Moore, and Burton, each with their own backgrounds steeped in conservative economic ideology, outline a vision that prioritizes deregulation, tax cuts for the wealthy, and market-driven solutions over comprehensive fiscal oversight and equitable economic growth. Their proposals reflect a drive to reshape the Department of the Treasury into an entity that aligns with corporate interests, raising significant concerns about the erosion of economic fairness and the neglect of the broader public welfare.

William Walton, a prominent figure in conservative circles, has long championed the cause of reducing government intervention in the economy. His tenure at various conservative think tanks has been marked by relentless advocacy for deregulation and tax cuts. Walton argues that these measures will spur economic growth, but his approach often disregards the negative consequences of such policies. Deregulation can lead to increased financial instability and unchecked corporate practices, while tax cuts for the wealthy exacerbate income inequality and reduce government revenue for public services.

Stephen Moore, a well-known conservative economist and commentator, has a history of promoting supply-side economics, a theory that suggests economic growth can be most effectively fostered by lowering taxes and decreasing regulation. During his time advising policymakers, Moore has pushed for significant tax cuts for corporations and high-income individuals. While he claims this will boost economic activity, the reality is that such policies often fail to deliver broad-based benefits and instead primarily enrich the already wealthy. Moore's vision neglects the importance of a balanced tax system that ensures all citizens contribute their fair share to the nation's needs.

David R. Burton, with his extensive experience in tax policy and fiscal regulation, has consistently advocated for reducing regulatory burdens on businesses. While reducing unnecessary regulation can indeed promote efficiency, Burton's approach tends to overlook the crucial role of regulations in protecting consumers, ensuring fair competition, and preventing financial crises. His push for deregulation can lead to an environment where short-term profits are prioritized over long-term stability and public trust.

Together, Walton, Moore, and Burton promote a strategy that significantly weakens the Treasury's ability to manage the economy effectively. Their collective emphasis on deregulation and tax cuts reflects a narrow focus on boosting corporate profits rather than fostering a fair and stable economic environment. This approach risks creating financial volatility and deepening economic inequality, ultimately harming the middle and lower-income segments of society the most. Their vision also includes a troubling push for privatization of government functions related to financial oversight and management. Privatization, they argue, will increase efficiency. Public oversight is crucial for ensuring that financial practices serve the broader public interest rather than just the interests of the wealthy and powerful.

Moreover, the trio's stance on reducing public spending as a means to balance the budget is deeply concerning. Cutting funding for healthcare, education, and social security to achieve budgetary goals can lead to widespread social harm and economic instability.

In summary, "The Economy: Department of the Treasury" by William Walton, Stephen Moore, and David R. Burton presents a vision for U.S. economic policy that prioritizes deregulation, tax cuts, and privatization. Their proposals for reducing federal oversight, promoting corporate interests, and cutting public spending reflect a troubling shift towards serving the wealthy at the expense of the broader population. This document serves as a warning of the potential dangers of prioritizing market efficiency and corporate profits over the fundamental goals of economic justice and social welfare, underscoring the need to preserve a balanced and fair approach to fiscal policy.

Why We Can't Trust William Walton

We cannot trust William Walton because his background and actions reveal a consistent pattern of prioritizing corporate interests and deregulation over the well-being of the broader public. As a prominent figure in conservative circles and a key player at various think tanks, Walton has long championed reducing government intervention in the economy. His relentless advocacy for deregulation and tax cuts for the wealthy often overlooks the severe negative consequences these policies can have on economic stability and social equity.

One notable example of Walton's controversial approach is his push for extensive tax cuts aimed at corporations and high-income individuals. He argues that these measures will spur economic growth, but history and research repeatedly show that such tax cuts primarily enrich the already wealthy and do little to benefit the broader economy. During his tenure influencing policymakers, Walton's policies have often led to increased income inequality and reduced government revenue, undermining the funding necessary for essential public services like healthcare, education, and infrastructure. His focus on benefiting the wealthy at the expense of the middle and lower classes makes his economic strategies deeply incredulous.

Organizations he supports have been at the forefront of efforts to defund Planned Parenthood, restrict access to reproductive healthcare, and roll back environmental protections. Walton's financial backing of these groups demonstrates a clear alignment with an agenda that seeks to control women's bodies and undermine their autonomy, as well as degrade environmental protections that are crucial for public health and combating climate change.

In summary, William Walton's past behavior, characterized by aggressive support for deregulation, funding of groups that undermine women's rights and environmental protections, and prioritization of corporate power, makes him a deeply outrageous and untrustworthy figure. His actions consistently prioritize radical conservative ideologies over the rights and welfare of ordinary Americans, particularly women and minorities. If given more influence, Walton's approach could lead to significant social and economic harm, exacerbating inequality and undermining democratic principles.

Why We Can't Trust Stephan Moore

We cannot trust Stephen Moore because his background and actions reveal a consistent pattern of promoting policies that favor the wealthy at the expense of broader economic stability and fairness. As a well-known conservative economist and commentator, Moore has been a leading advocate of supply-side economics, a theory that suggests economic growth can be most effectively fostered by lowering taxes and reducing regulation. His tenure advising policymakers, particularly during the Trump administration, has seen the implementation of significant tax cuts for corporations and high-income individuals, measures that have primarily enriched the wealthy while failing to deliver the promised broad-based economic benefits.

One notable example of Moore's controversial approach is his staunch support for the Tax Cuts and Jobs Act of 2017. Moore argued that these tax cuts would spur economic growth and benefit all Americans. However, the reality has been quite different. The bulk of the benefits from these tax cuts have gone to the wealthy and large corporations, leading to increased income inequality. Additionally, the reduction in federal revenue has contributed to ballooning deficits, putting pressure on funding for essential public services like education, healthcare, and infrastructure. Moore's insistence on tax cuts as a panacea for economic issues overlooks the complexities of fiscal policy and the need for balanced revenue sources to support a healthy economy.

Moreover, Moore's advocacy for deregulation poses significant risks to economic and environmental stability. He has steadily argued the Reaganomic myth that reducing regulatory burdens will foster innovation and growth. However, his approach fails to acknowledge the critical role of regulations in safeguarding public health, protecting consumers, and ensuring fair market practices. Deregulation can lead to financial instability, as seen in the lead-up to the 2008 financial crisis, and environmental degradation, as corporations cut corners to maximize profits. Moore's background and actions suggest a willingness to prioritize short-term economic gains for the wealthy over long-term stability and equity, making his policies and intentions deeply untrustworthy.

Why We Can't Trust David R. Burton

We cannot trust David R. Burton because his background and actions reveal a consistent pattern of prioritizing corporate interests and deregulation over the protections necessary for consumers, workers, and the environment. As a senior fellow at The Heritage Foundation and a prominent figure in tax and fiscal policy, Burton has been a vocal advocate for reducing regulatory burdens on businesses, claiming this will spur economic growth. However, his approach often overlooks the critical role of regulations in ensuring fair practices and preventing financial crises.

One notable example of Burton's controversial approach is his support for the extensive deregulation of financial markets. He falsely pushes the lie that reducing regulatory oversight will enhance efficiency and innovation in the financial sector. This perspective, however, fails to acknowledge the lessons from the 2008 financial crisis, where insufficient oversight led to reckless behavior, severe economic fallout, and devastating consequences for ordinary citizens. By pushing for deregulation, Burton risks repeating these mistakes, potentially leading to financial instability and the exploitation of consumers. His tenure at The Heritage Foundation has been marked by a consistent push to dismantle regulatory safeguards that protect the public from corporate malfeasance.

Moreover, Burton's stance on tax policy further highlights his problematic approach. He has consistently advocated for significant tax cuts for corporations and the wealthy, arguing that such measures will generate broad economic benefits. In reality, these policies often exacerbate income inequality and reduce government revenue, undermining the funding necessary for essential public services like healthcare, education, and infrastructure. Burton's proposals frequently prioritize the interests of the wealthy over the needs of the broader population, contributing to a growing economic divide. His background and actions suggest a willingness to sacrifice public welfare for corporate profits and ideological purity, making his policies and intentions deeply untrustworthy. His vision for economic policy undermines the balanced and comprehensive oversight needed to ensure a fair and just economy for all.

Section 4:
The Economy
23 Export-Import Bank
The Export-Import Bank Should Be Abolished
by Veronique de Rugy

- A Cautionary Tale

Folks, brace yourselves, because the tale you are about to hear will leave you in fear. "The Economy: Export-Import Bank: The Export-Import Bank Should be Abolished," by Veronique de Rugy is an unsettling fervent argument for the abolition of the Export-Import Bank, presenting it as a flawed institution riddled with inefficiency and favoritism. While her arguments are compelling, they also reveal deeper issues that raise critical concerns about the true impact of the Ex-Im Bank on the economy and society.

De Rugy begins by highlighting how the Ex-Im Bank predominantly benefits large corporations like Boeing and General Electric. These well-established giants hardly need government support to compete globally. By channeling vast amounts of resources to these companies, the bank distorts market dynamics, creating an uneven playing field that disadvantages smaller, innovative businesses. This favoritism fosters a form of corporate welfare, where government support is not equitably distributed.

Moreover, de Rugy emphasizes the significant financial risks posed to taxpayers by the Ex-Im Bank's operations. The loans and guarantees provided by the bank are backed by public funds, meaning that any defaults directly impact taxpayers. Given the volatile nature of international markets, the risk of defaults is far from negligible. The potential for substantial financial losses makes the bank's operations a reckless gamble with public money, a point that de Rugy drives home with alarming clarity.

De Rugy also critiques the economic distortions caused by the Ex-Im Bank's selective support. By favoring certain industries and companies, the bank disrupts the natural allocation of capital, leading to inefficiencies and stifling competition. This selective support not only hampers broader economic growth but also limits innovation, as resources are funneled towards already dominant players rather than fostering a diverse and competitive market.

The issues of corruption and mismanagement within the Ex-Im Bank are also highlighted. De Rugy documents instances of fraud and inefficiency, leading to a waste of taxpayer dollars and eroding public trust. She argues that abolishing the bank would eliminate a significant source of government corruption and ensure that public funds are used more effectively and transparently.

Furthermore, de Rugy contends that the foundational rationale for the Ex-Im Bank is outdated. In today's global economy, private financial institutions are fully capable of providing the necessary export financing services. The private sector's ability to meet these needs efficiently renders the government's role redundant. De Rugy suggests that the Ex-Im Bank is an unnecessary relic that no longer serves a vital purpose.

The argument that the Ex-Im Bank is necessary to counter foreign subsidies is also dismantled. Engaging in subsidy wars, de Rugy argues, perpetuates a cycle of dependency and economic distortion. Instead, the U.S. should lead efforts to eliminate such subsidies globally, promoting fairer and more sustainable trade practices. This approach, she asserts, would benefit the economy far more than maintaining a costly and inefficient government agency.

In summary, "The Economy: Export-Import Bank: The Export-Import Bank Should Be Abolished" by Veronique de Rugy's presents a compelling case for the abolition of the Export-Import Bank. She portrays the bank as a facilitator of corporate welfare, a financial risk to taxpayers, and a source of economic distortion and corruption. By dismantling the Ex-Im Bank, de Rugy argues, the U.S. can save taxpayer money, promote fair competition, and foster a more equitable and efficient economic environment. This vision underscores the need for a thorough reevaluation of government involvement in economic affairs, emphasizing transparency, accountability, and fairness.

Why We Can't Trust Veronique de Rugy

We cannot trust Veronique de Rugy because her background and actions reveal a consistent pattern of promoting extreme free-market ideologies that often overlook the complexities and nuances of economic realities. As a senior research fellow at the Mercatus Center, a think tank known for its libertarian leanings, de Rugy has been a vocal advocate for minimal government intervention in the economy. While this perspective can have merits, her rigid adherence to deregulation and reduced government roles often disregards the essential protections and support systems needed for a balanced and fair economy.

One notable example of de Rugy's controversial stance is her persistent call for the abolition of the Export-Import Bank. She argues that the bank distorts the market and favors large corporations, but her analysis frequently neglects the broader benefits that the bank provides, especially to small and medium-sized enterprises (SMEs). The Ex-Im Bank plays a crucial role in leveling the playing field for these businesses, which often lack the resources to secure private financing for international trade. By focusing solely on the potential downsides, de Rugy fails to acknowledge how the bank supports job creation and economic growth among smaller businesses.

Moreover, de Rugy's unwavering support for extensive deregulation can lead to significant risks. Her background at the Mercatus Center involves advocating for policies that reduce oversight and accountability in various sectors. This approach, while theoretically promoting economic efficiency, can result in unintended consequences such as financial instability, environmental degradation, and increased inequality. For instance, the financial crisis of 2008 demonstrated the dangers of insufficient regulation in the banking sector, yet de Rugy's proposals often overlook these critical lessons, favoring an overly simplistic view of market self-regulation.

In summary, Veronique de Rugy's background and actions suggest a commitment to extreme free-market principles that can undermine essential economic protections and support systems. This makes her perspectives and recommendations deeply deluded and untrustworthy, as they prioritize ideological purity over pragmatic solutions that benefit the broader economy.

118

Section 4:
The Economy
23 Export-Import Bank
The Case for the Export-Import Bank
by Jennifer Hazelton

- *A Cautionary Tale*

Pay close attention, everyone, because what is about to be disclosed is frightening beyond belief. "The Economy: Export-Import Bank: The Export-Import Bank Should Not Be Abolished," by Jennifer Hazelton presents a case for retaining the Export-Import Bank (Ex-Im Bank) as an essential tool for supporting American exporters. While Hazelton argues persuasively for the bank's continued existence, her analysis falls short by not addressing the deep-seated issues that necessitate significant reforms.

Hazelton begins by emphasizing the Ex-Im Bank's role in leveling the playing field for U.S. businesses against foreign competitors who receive substantial government backing. However, she overlooks the fact that perpetuating subsidy wars only deepens economic distortions and dependencies. Instead of justifying the bank's existence, a more critical approach would call for international agreements to reduce such subsidies, fostering a genuinely fair competitive environment.

The chapter highlights the Ex-Im Bank's importance to small and medium-sized enterprises (SMEs), suggesting that the bank provides crucial support for these businesses to expand internationally. While SMEs do benefit, Hazelton fails to acknowledge that a disproportionate amount of the bank's resources still goes to large corporations like Boeing and General Electric. To truly support SMEs, reforms should include capping the percentage of funds allocated to large corporations and increasing transparency in how financial assistance is distributed.

Hazelton asserts that the Ex-Im Bank operates at a profit and has a low default rate, presenting it as a low-risk institution. Yet, the risk to taxpayers remains substantial, especially in volatile international markets. Hazelton's argument would be stronger if it included measures to safeguard taxpayer money, such as stricter lending criteria and enhanced risk assessment protocols.

While Hazelton claims the Ex-Im Bank supports thousands of jobs across various sectors, this view ignores the broader economic distortions created by selective government support. True economic growth and job creation come from fostering a competitive and innovative market environment. Reforms should focus on ensuring that the bank's support does not inadvertently stifle competition by unfairly favoring certain industries over others.

The chapter acknowledges issues of corruption and inefficiency within the Ex-Im Bank but suggests that mere reforms will suffice. This underestimates the systemic nature of these problems. Effective reforms would require not only stronger oversight but also independent audits and whistleblower protections to root out corruption and improve operational efficiency.

Hazelton's argument that the Ex-Im Bank is strategically important for national security and economic resilience is valid. However, she fails to address the potential for the bank to be misused for corporate cronyism rather than genuine national interest. Reforms should include clear guidelines and accountability measures to ensure that the bank's activities align with national security goals and public interest rather than corporate agendas.

Lastly, Hazelton dismisses the notion that private financial institutions could replace the Ex-Im Bank's functions, arguing that the bank's unique ability to mitigate risks is unmatched. While the private sector may not entirely replace the bank, incorporating private sector practices in risk management and customer service can enhance the bank's efficiency and effectiveness.

In conclusion, "The Economy: Export-Import Bank: The Case for the Export-Import Bank" by Jennifer Hazelton's defends the Export-Import Bank's continued existence, it glosses over significant issues that demand reform. To ensure the bank serves its intended purpose without perpetuating corporate welfare or exposing taxpayers to undue risk, comprehensive reforms are necessary. These should include capping support for large corporations, improving transparency, enhancing risk management, and implementing stringent oversight mechanisms. Only then can the Ex-Im Bank truly fulfill its mission in a fair and effective manner.

Why We Can't Trust Jennifer Hazelton

We cannot trust Jennifer Hazelton because her background and actions reveal a consistent pattern of promoting policies that favor corporate interests and ideological agendas over the broader public good. As a former communications director for the Trump campaign and a senior advisor at the Heritage Foundation, Hazelton has been deeply involved in crafting and advocating for policies that prioritize deregulation and privatization. These policies often overlook the essential protections and support systems needed to ensure fairness and stability in the economy.

One notable example of Hazelton's controversial approach is her defense of the Export-Import Bank. While she argues that the bank is crucial for supporting U.S. exporters, her perspective tends to emphasize the benefits to large corporations like Boeing and General Electric. These companies, which already have significant resources, receive the majority of the bank's support, creating an uneven playing field that disadvantages smaller businesses. Hazelton's background in promoting policies that favor big business at the expense of small enterprises and the broader public raises concerns about her true motivations and priorities.

Moreover, Hazelton's advocacy for extensive deregulation poses significant risks to economic and environmental stability. Her background at the Heritage Foundation involves pushing for reduced oversight and accountability across various sectors, under the guise of promoting economic growth. This approach, while theoretically increasing efficiency, can lead to significant negative consequences such as financial instability, environmental degradation, and increased inequality. The 2008 financial crisis is a stark reminder of the dangers of insufficient regulation, yet Hazelton's proposals often fail to address these critical lessons, favoring an overly simplistic view of market self-regulation.

In summary, Jennifer Hazelton's background and actions suggest a commitment to corporate interests and ideological purity over the public good. This makes her perspectives and recommendations deeply delusional and untrustworthy, as they prioritize ideological agendas over pragmatic solutions that benefit the broader economy.

Section 4:
The Economy
24 Federal Reserve
by Paul Winfree

- A Cautionary Tale

Come near, folks, for the story you are about to hear is more chilling
than you can imagine. "The Economy: Federal Reserve" by Paul
Winfree outlines a vision for fundamentally transforming the Federal
Reserve's role in the American economy. Winfree's proposals, while
presented with an air of reform and efficiency, hide a myriad of risks
and potential downfalls that could have far-reaching consequences for
economic stability and public welfare.

Winfree begins by advocating for a significant reduction in the
Federal Reserve's regulatory authority. He argues that the current
regulatory framework stifles economic growth and innovation. While
it's true that overregulation can hinder business activity, Winfree's
sweeping call for deregulation overlooks the essential role that
financial regulations play in maintaining economic stability and
protecting consumers. The 2008 financial crisis starkly illustrated the
dangers of insufficient oversight, leading to widespread economic
turmoil. Reducing the Fed's regulatory powers risks repeating these
catastrophic mistakes, paving the way for another financial meltdown.

Moreover, Winfree suggests that the Federal Reserve should focus
primarily on controlling inflation, rather than pursuing a dual
mandate that includes maximizing employment. This narrow focus
on inflation control ignores the complex interplay between inflation
and employment. The dual mandate exists because both inflation and
employment are crucial for economic stability. By sidelining the
employment aspect, Winfree's proposals could lead to higher
unemployment rates and exacerbate economic inequality, creating
hardship for working families and increasing the economic divide.

Winfree also calls for a return to more traditional monetary policies,
such as tightening the money supply to combat inflation. While
controlling inflation is important, doing so at the expense of economic
growth can be dangerous. During economic downturns, flexible

monetary policies are vital for stimulating growth and preventing prolonged recessions. Winfree's rigid adherence to traditional policies may limit the Fed's ability to respond effectively to economic crises, potentially leading to slower recoveries and more profound economic hardship.

The chapter emphasizes the need for greater transparency and accountability within the Federal Reserve. Winfree proposes increasing political oversight as a means to achieve this. However, this approach risks undermining the Fed's independence, which is crucial for making unbiased economic decisions. Increased political influence could lead to short-term policymaking driven by political agendas rather than long-term economic stability. Such pressures could destabilize the economy by prioritizing immediate political gains over sound economic policies.

Winfree's vision includes ending the Federal Reserve's role in backstopping financial institutions during crises, arguing that this would reduce moral hazard and encourage more prudent behavior among banks. This perspective fails to recognize the critical role that the Fed plays in preventing systemic collapses. The intervention of the Fed during the 2008 financial crisis, though controversial, was essential in stabilizing the financial system and preventing a deeper economic depression. Removing this safety net could lead to more severe economic downturns in the future, putting the entire economy at risk.

Another brazen aspect of Winfree's proposals is the push for further deregulation in the financial sector. While deregulation can spur economic growth, it often leads to increased risk-taking and instability. The deregulation efforts of the late 20th century significantly contributed to the 2008 financial crisis. Winfree's vision risks repeating past mistakes and undermining the safeguards that protect the economy from excessive risk and financial crises.

In summary, "The Economy: Federal Reserve" by Paul Winfree presents a vision for the Federal Reserve that emphasizes deregulation, minimizing the complex nature of policymaking, a balanced and nuanced approach is necessary to ensure that the Federal Reserve can effectively promote economic stability and prosperity for all Americans.

Why We Can't Trust Paul Winfree

We cannot trust Paul Winfree because his background and actions reveal a consistent pattern of advocating for policies that prioritize deregulation and reduced government oversight, often at the expense of economic stability and public welfare. As a former director of budget policy at the Heritage Foundation and a key economic advisor in the Trump administration, Winfree has championed limiting the Federal Reserve's regulatory authority, overlooking the way financial regulations work in maintaining stability and protecting consumers.

One significant example of Winfree's controversial stance is his support for narrowing the Federal Reserve's focus to primarily controlling inflation, sidelining its dual mandate to also maximize employment. During his tenure at the Heritage Foundation, Winfree promoted policies that emphasized strict inflation control over broader economic health. This narrow focus can lead to higher unemployment and greater economic inequality, as it neglects the complex interplay between inflation and employment. By advocating for a singular focus on inflation, Winfree risks exacerbating economic disparities and ignoring the needs of the broader workforce.

Moreover, Winfree's push for increased political oversight of the Federal Reserve raises significant concerns. He argues that greater transparency and accountability can be achieved through more political influence over the Fed's decision-making processes. However, this approach undermines the Fed's independence, a critical component for making unbiased economic decisions. Political pressures could result in short-term policymaking that prioritizes immediate gains over long-term stability.

Furthermore, his tenure in the Trump administration saw numerous efforts to roll back regulations across various sectors, often without adequate consideration of the potential risks. The deregulation efforts of the late 20th century, which significantly contributed to the 2008 financial crisis, underscore the dangers of such an approach. Winfree's failure to acknowledge these lessons and his push for further deregulation demonstrate a disregard for the safeguards necessary to protect the economy from excessive risk and instability. His background and actions indicate a preference for ideological purity over pragmatic solutions, making his voice on policies highly suspect.

Section 4:
The Economy
25 Small Business Administration
by Karen Kerrigan

- A Cautionary Tale

Lean in, everyone, Because this story is sure to make your blood run cold. "The Economy: Small Business Association," by Karen Kerrigan, presents a vision that aims to support and uplift small businesses. However, a critical examination reveals that her proposals may undermine the very foundations that ensure fair competition, equitable support, and the protection of vulnerable businesses. Kerrigan, known for her advocacy for small businesses, presents a perspective that, while well-intentioned, overlooks key aspects that are crucial for a balanced and effective small business ecosystem.

Kerrigan begins by emphasizing the need for deregulation to foster a more favorable environment for small businesses. She argues that excessive regulations stifle innovation and growth, presenting a significant burden for small business owners. While it's true that some regulations can be cumbersome, Kerrigan's sweeping call for deregulation fails to consider the protective role these regulations play. Regulations are often in place to ensure fair competition, protect consumers, and safeguard the environment. Eliminating these protections can lead to a race to the bottom, where only the most unscrupulous businesses thrive, ultimately harming the broader small business community.

Moreover, Kerrigan advocates for reducing the role of the SBA in providing direct loans and instead suggests that private financial institutions should take on this responsibility. This perspective overlooks the crucial role the SBA plays in supporting businesses that might not otherwise have access to necessary capital. The private sector often prioritizes profit over equity, leading to the exclusion of many deserving small businesses, especially those in underserved communities. By reducing the SBA's direct involvement, Kerrigan risks exacerbating existing disparities and leaving many small businesses without the support they need to grow and thrive.

Kerrigan also highlights the importance of tax cuts for small businesses, arguing that lower taxes will spur investment and growth. While lower taxes can indeed provide immediate financial relief, this approach fails to address the root issues that many small businesses face, such as access to affordable healthcare, workforce development, and market competition. A comprehensive strategy that includes targeted tax relief alongside investments in these critical areas would be more effective in promoting sustainable growth for small businesses.

The chapter's call for increased privatization of SBA services raises additional concerns. Kerrigan suggests that private entities can deliver these services more efficiently. However, this perspective often ignores the profit motives of private firms, which can lead to higher costs and reduced service quality. The SBA's role as a government agency is to serve the public interest, ensuring that small businesses receive equitable support. Privatization risks transforming these services into profit-driven ventures that may not prioritize the needs of the small business community.

Furthermore, Kerrigan's proposals for streamlining the SBA's operations and reducing its budget are problematic. While efficiency is important, drastic budget cuts can undermine the agency's ability to provide essential support services. The SBA's mission is to foster small business growth and development, and adequate funding is crucial for it to fulfill this mission effectively. Reducing the budget could lead to a reduction in critical programs and services that many small businesses rely on. Kerrigan also downplays the importance of the SBA's role in disaster recovery and assistance. The agency's involvement in providing support during and after disasters is vital for helping small businesses recover and rebuild. Reducing the SBA's capacity in this area would leave many businesses vulnerable in times of crisis, undermining economic resilience and stability.

In conclusion, "The Economy: Small Business Administration" by Karen Kerrigan advocates for a more deregulated and privatized approach to supporting small businesses, it overlooks the protective and equitable roles that the SBA plays. Her proposals would lead to disparities, reduced support for vulnerable businesses, and a weakening of the safety nets that are crucial for fostering a healthy and competitive small business environment.

Why We Can't Trust Karen Kerrigan

We cannot trust Karen Kerrigan because her background and actions consistently advocate for policies prioritizing deregulation and privatization, often overlooking critical protections and support systems small businesses need. As president and CEO of the Small Business & Entrepreneurship Council, Kerrigan pushes for reduced government intervention, which, though sometimes beneficial, can lead to significant issues without necessary oversight. Her strong advocacy for deregulation argues that excessive regulations stifle small business growth. While reducing red tape is valid, her broad deregulation push overlooks protections ensuring fair competition, consumer safety, and environmental safeguards. This could allow unscrupulous businesses to exploit gaps, ultimately harming the small business community.

Kerrigan's push to privatize services provided by the Small Business Administration (SBA) raises concerns. She believes private entities can offer these services more efficiently. However, this often overlooks the profit motives of private entities, potentially leading to higher costs and reduced service quality. The SBA ensures equitable support, especially for businesses less attractive to the private sector due to higher risk or lower profitability. By advocating for privatization, Kerrigan risks exacerbating existing disparities and leaving many small businesses without the support they need to grow and thrive.

Lastly, Kerrigan advocates for substantial tax cuts for small businesses, arguing this will spur growth. While lower taxes provide immediate relief, they don't address underlying issues like access to affordable healthcare and workforce development. A more comprehensive strategy balancing tax relief with investments in critical areas would better promote sustainable growth. In summary, Karen Kerrigan's background and actions show a preference for policies prioritizing deregulation and privatization without considering the protective roles of government regulations and support systems. Her recommendations, while aiming to support small businesses, risk undermining the foundations necessary for a competitive small business environment, making her approach deeply traitorous to the public and untrustworthy.

Section 4:
The Economy
26 Trade: The Case for Fair Trade
by Peter Navarro

- A Cautionary Tale

Listen carefully, folks, because what is about to be revealed is deeply unsettling. "The Economy: Trade: The Case for Fair Trade," by Peter Navarro outlines a plan that seeks to protect American jobs and industries through aggressive trade policies. While his intentions to bolster the U.S. economy are clear, the proposals are fraught with economic isolationism, trade wars, and unintended consequences.

Navarro begins by highlighting the unfair practices of foreign competitors, such as currency manipulation, state subsidies, and labor exploitation. He argues that these practices undermine American businesses and necessitate a robust response. However, his approach leans dangerously towards protectionism, which can provoke retaliation from trading partners. This could spiral into trade wars, threatening global economic stability and harming U.S. interests. Navarro's strategy is perilously short-sighted, ignoring the complex interdependencies of the global economy.

One of the most alarming aspects of Navarro's plan is his reliance on tariffs as a primary tool for enforcing fair trade. While tariffs might protect certain industries in the short term, they often lead to higher prices for consumers and strained international relationships. Retaliatory tariffs could severely hurt American exporters, leading to job losses in sectors dependent on foreign markets. Navarro's emphasis on tariffs risks creating a hostile trade environment that could undermine the very economic growth and job security he seeks to achieve.

Moreover, Navarro's perspective dismisses the benefits of globalization and multilateral trade agreements. While it is true that not all sectors have benefited equally, free trade has generally fostered economic growth, innovation, and consumer choice. By focusing solely on the negatives, Navarro's strategy risks alienating allies and reducing opportunities for cooperative solutions to trade imbalances. A more balanced approach would involve working with international partners through multilateral agreements rather than unilateral measures, which might provoke further economic instability.

Navarro stresses the need for stringent enforcement of trade rules to ensure fair competition. While enforcement is crucial, his proposals often lack the nuance required to address complex trade issues. Overzealous enforcement could lead to supply chain disruptions and increased costs for businesses that rely on imported materials. A more effective strategy would combine targeted enforcement with diplomatic efforts to address the root causes of unfair trade practices, rather than imposing blanket measures that might backfire.

Navarro's push for reshoring manufacturing jobs to the United States is another troubling aspect of his plan. While the idea of bringing jobs back home sounds appealing, it overlooks the reality of modern manufacturing, which relies heavily on automation and advanced technologies. While reshoring might bring back some jobs, it is unlikely to result in the large-scale employment gains Navarro promises. Policies should instead focus on workforce development and education, preparing workers for the jobs of the future and ensuring they have the skills needed to thrive in a rapidly changing economy.

Navarro's proposals also raise concerns about their potential impact on developing countries. By imposing strict trade barriers, the United States could inadvertently harm the economies of developing nations that rely on exports to sustain their growth. This could lead to increased global inequality and instability, undermining long-term global economic progress and contradicting the goals of promoting fair trade and economic justice.

In conclusion, "The Economy: The Case for Fair Trade" by Peter Navarro makes a compelling case for addressing unfair trade practices, but his reliance on protectionist measures and tariffs risks provoking trade wars and economic isolationism. A more balanced approach, including multilateral cooperation, targeted enforcement, and investments in workforce development, would be more effective in promoting fair trade and ensuring long-term economic stability. Navarro's proposals, while well-intentioned, require critical reevaluation to avoid unintended consequences that could ultimately undermine their goals and leave the U.S. economy vulnerable to new and unpredictable dangers.

Why We Can't Trust Peter Navarro

We cannot trust Peter Navarro because his background and actions consistently reveal a tendency towards extreme economic policies that prioritize protectionism over balanced trade and global cooperation. As a former advisor to President Trump, Navarro was a key architect of aggressive trade policies that led to economic instability and strained international relationships. His academic background, while extensive, often emphasizes theoretical approaches that do not always translate effectively into practical policy.

One significant example of Navarro's controversial stance is his unwavering support for tariffs. During his tenure, Navarro was instrumental in implementing tariffs on imports from China and other countries. These tariffs, intended to protect American industries, resulted in higher costs for consumers and retaliatory measures from affected countries. The ensuing trade wars hurt American farmers and manufacturers, disrupting global supply chains and creating economic uncertainty. Navarro's approach often disregards the benefits of globalization and multilateral trade agreements. His preference for unilateral measures and bilateral agreements undermines established international trade norms and alienates key allies. For instance, his opposition to the Trans-Pacific Partnership (TPP) ignored the potential benefits of a multilateral approach to addressing trade imbalances with China.

In summary, Navarro's push for reshoring manufacturing jobs to the U.S. overlooks the complexities of modern manufacturing, which relies heavily on automation and advanced technologies. His promises of large-scale employment gains fail to account for the evolving nature of manufacturing jobs, requiring different skills than those lost to offshoring. His failure to grasp these nuances indicates a limited understanding of contemporary economic dynamics and workforce needs. Navarro's proposals also raise concerns about their impact on developing countries. By imposing strict trade barriers, the U.S. might inadvertently harm economies that depend on exports for growth, leading to increased global inequality and instability. A more balanced approach, including multilateral cooperation, targeted enforcement, and investments in workforce development, would be more effective in promoting fair trade and ensuring economic stability compared to his limited understanding of dynamic economics.

Section 4:
The Economy
26 Trade: The Case for Free Trade
by Kent Lassman

- A Cautionary Tale

Gather 'round, all, for the events that are about to be recounted are truly terrifying. "The Economy" Trade: The Case for Free Trade," by Kent Lassman paints a deeply distressing vision for American trade policy, advocating for a radical shift towards unrestrained free trade. While Lassman presents his ideas as a means to foster economic growth and innovation, his proposals carry terrifying risks of economic inequality, exploitation, and the erosion of critical protections for workers and the environment.

Lassman begins by extolling the virtues of free trade, arguing that reducing trade barriers and opening markets will lead to increased economic efficiency, lower prices for consumers, and greater innovation. However, this overly optimistic view ignores the harsh realities of unregulated global trade. Without appropriate safeguards, free trade can exacerbate economic inequalities, leading to job losses in vulnerable industries and regions. Lassman's vision fails to address the social and economic costs of such disruptions, particularly for workers who may be left behind in a rapidly changing global economy.

One of the most alarming aspects of Lassman's plan is his call for the dismantling of trade barriers and tariffs without adequate consideration of their protective roles. While reducing tariffs can indeed lower costs and stimulate trade, it also opens domestic industries to intense competition from countries with lower labor standards and weaker environmental regulations. This can lead to a race to the bottom, where businesses cut corners to remain competitive, resulting in poorer working conditions and increased environmental degradation. Lassman's disregard for these critical issues reflects a dangerous naivety about the complex interplay between trade, labor, and environmental standards.

Moreover, Lassman's emphasis on the theoretical benefits of free trade overlooks the practical challenges faced by many countries. He suggests that all nations will benefit equally from open markets, but this ignores the significant power imbalances that exist in global trade relationships. Wealthier countries often have more leverage in negotiations, which can lead to trade deals that disproportionately benefit them at the expense of poorer nations. Lassman's proposals risk entrenching these inequalities, further marginalizing already disadvantaged populations and exacerbating global economic disparities.

Lassman also fails to adequately address the impact of free trade on local economies and communities. While he champions the idea that consumers will benefit from lower prices and greater choice, he ignores the potential for local businesses to be driven out of the market by larger multinational corporations. This can lead to the hollowing out of local economies, with devastating social and economic consequences. Lassman's vision of unrestrained free trade does not account for the need to support and protect local businesses and communities from the disruptive forces of global competition.

Another deeply typical Reaganomic aspect of Lassman's proposals is his dismissal of the need for robust regulatory frameworks to manage the effects of free trade. He argues that market forces alone will ensure fair outcomes, but this ignores the historical evidence of market failures and abuses. Without strong regulations, there is a significant risk that free trade will lead to exploitation, environmental harm, and economic instability. Lassman's faith in the self-regulating power of markets is dangerously misplaced and ignores the critical role of government oversight in protecting public interests.

In summary, "The Economy: The Case for Free Trade" by Kent Lassman advocates for a radical shift towards unrestrained free trade, but his proposals carry significant risks. By ignoring the social, economic, and environmental costs of such a shift, Lassman's vision threatens to exacerbate inequality, exploitation, and instability. A more balanced approach, incorporating robust regulatory frameworks and protections for workers and the environment, is essential to ensure that the benefits of free trade are shared equitably and sustainably. Lassman's proposals, while aiming to promote economic growth, require a critical reevaluation to avoid unintended consequences that could undermine their goals and leave vulnerable populations at risk.

Why We Can't Trust Kent Lassman

We cannot trust Kent Lassman because his background and actions reveal a consistent pattern of advocating for extreme free-market policies that often disregard the social and economic protections necessary for a fair and stable economy. As president and CEO of the Competitive Enterprise Institute (CEI), Lassman has been a vocal proponent of deregulation and unrestrained free trade, prioritizing corporate interests over the well-being of workers and the environment.

One significant example of Lassman's controversial stance is his strong opposition to regulatory frameworks that protect labor and environmental standards. At CEI, Lassman has pushed for the dismantling of regulations he views as barriers to economic growth. However, this approach often overlooks the critical role these regulations play in ensuring fair labor practices and environmental sustainability. By advocating for reduced oversight, Lassman's policies risk exacerbating worker exploitation and environmental degradation, as businesses cut corners to remain competitive in an unregulated market. Lassman's emphasis on the theoretical benefits of free trade fails to account for the practical challenges and inequalities inherent in global trade. He argues that reducing trade barriers will lead to widespread economic benefits, but this perspective ignores the significant power imbalances that favor wealthier nations and multinational corporations. During his tenure at CEI, Lassman has consistently supported trade policies that benefit large corporations while neglecting the adverse impacts on smaller businesses and vulnerable communities. This focus on corporate interests undermines the equitable distribution of trade benefits and exacerbates economic disparities.

In summary, Kent Lassman's background and actions indicate a preference for extreme free-market policies that prioritize deregulation and unrestrained free trade without considering the essential protections for workers and the environment. By ignoring the complex realities of global trade and the need for balanced regulatory frameworks, Lassman's policies risk exacerbating economic inequality and instability, making them unsuitable for ensuring a fair and sustainable economy.

Section 5:
Independent Regulatory Agencies
27 Financial Regulatory Agencies:
Securities and Exchange Commission & Related Agencies
by David R. Burton

- A Cautionary Tale

Friends, hold your breath, because what you are about to hear will leave you in terror. "Independent Regulatory Agencies: Financial Regulatory Agencies & Securities and Exchange Commission & Related Agencies," by David R. Burton presents a daunting vision for reforming financial regulation. While Burton aims to streamline these agencies to promote economic efficiency, his proposals carry significant risks of financial instability, reduced consumer protections, and increased corporate malfeasance.

Burton begins by arguing that financial regulatory agencies, including the Securities and Exchange Commission (SEC), impose excessive burdens on businesses, stifling innovation and growth. He advocates for substantial deregulation to foster a more business-friendly environment. However, this perspective dangerously underestimates the critical role these agencies play in maintaining market stability and protecting consumers. By pushing for deregulation, Burton risks repeating the mistakes that led to the 2008 financial crisis, where insufficient oversight allowed reckless behavior to flourish, ultimately causing widespread economic devastation.

One of Burton's alarming proposals is to reduce the independence of financial regulatory agencies by increasing political oversight. While he argues that this would enhance accountability, it threatens to undermine the objectivity and effectiveness of these agencies. Political influence could lead to short-term decision-making driven by electoral cycles rather than long-term economic stability. Burton's vision risks turning regulatory agencies into tools for political agendas, compromising their ability to regulate impartially and effectively.

Moreover, Burton's call for scaling back enforcement capabilities of agencies like the SEC is deeply telling. He suggests that aggressive enforcement actions hinder business operations and innovation.

However, robust enforcement is essential to deter fraud, insider trading, and other financial crimes. Weakening these enforcement capabilities would embolden bad actors, increasing the likelihood of financial misconduct and eroding public trust in the financial system. Burton's proposals could open the floodgates for corporate malfeasance, with devastating consequences for investors and the broader economy.

Burton also advocates for simplifying and reducing regulatory requirements, arguing that the current framework is overly complex and costly. While regulatory simplification can improve efficiency, overly broad deregulation can remove essential safeguards. For instance, post-crisis reforms like the Dodd-Frank Act introduced crucial measures to prevent another financial meltdown. Dismantling such protections without carefully considering their importance could leave the financial system vulnerable to new crises. Burton's proposals, though aimed at reducing costs, could ultimately impose far greater economic costs through increased instability.

Furthermore, Burton's focus on reducing regulatory costs for businesses often overlooks the benefits these regulations provide to consumers and the economy as a whole. Consumer protection regulations ensure that financial products and services are fair, transparent, and safe. Reducing these protections in the name of cost-cutting could expose consumers to predatory practices, financial scams, and significant financial harm. Burton's vision of a leaner regulatory framework fails to account for the vital consumer safeguards that prevent exploitation and financial distress. Burton also downplays the importance of regulatory agencies in maintaining global financial stability. Burton's proposals risk isolating the U.S. from global regulatory standards, potentially leading to global conflict.

In conclusion, "Independent Regulatory Agencies: Financial Regulatory Agencies, Securities and Exchange Commission, & Related Agencies" by David R. Burton advocates for deregulating financial regulatory agencies and carry significant risks. A more balanced approach, maintaining essential safeguards while improving regulatory efficiency, is necessary to ensure a stable and fair financial system. Burton's vision, while aiming for economic efficiency, requires critical reevaluation to avoid unintended consequences that could undermine financial stability and public trust.

Why We Can't Trust David R. Burton

We cannot trust David R. Burton because his background and actions consistently advocate for extreme deregulation and reduced government oversight, often ignoring the critical protections necessary for economic stability and consumer safety. As a senior fellow at the Heritage Foundation, Burton has been a vocal proponent of dismantling regulatory frameworks that protect the financial system and consumers from abuses and crises.

One significant example of Burton's controversial stance is his persistent call for reducing the independence and enforcement capabilities of financial regulatory agencies like the Securities and Exchange Commission (SEC). Burton argues that increased political oversight would enhance accountability, but this approach threatens to compromise the objectivity and effectiveness of these agencies. During his tenure at the Heritage Foundation, Burton has consistently pushed for policies that prioritize short-term business interests over long-term economic stability. His proposals risk turning regulatory agencies into tools for political agendas, which could lead to a repeat of the regulatory failures that contributed to the 2008 financial crisis.

Moreover, Burton's advocacy for deregulation often overlooks the essential role that regulations play in protecting consumers and ensuring market integrity. He argues that regulatory requirements are overly complex and costly, yet these very regulations are what prevent financial misconduct, fraud, and abuse. By calling for the dismantling of critical safeguards introduced by reforms like the Dodd-Frank Act, Burton's approach could expose the financial system to new vulnerabilities and crises.

In summary, David R. Burton's background and actions demonstrate a clear preference for deregulation and reduced oversight without adequately considering the essential protections provided by these frameworks. His proposals, while aimed at promoting economic efficiency, risk undermining financial stability, enabling corporate malfeasance, and leaving consumers vulnerable. Burton's policies reflect an untrustworthy approach that prioritizes short-term gains over the long-term health and integrity of the financial system, making his recommendations deeply unscrupulous and harmful.

Section 5:
Independent Regulatory Agencies
27 Financial Regulatory Agencies:
Consumer Protection Bureau
by Robert Bowes

- A Cautionary Tale

Alright, folks, gather close, because the story you are about to hear is nothing short of terrifying. "Independent Regulatory Agencies: Consumer Protection Agency," by Robert Bowes paints a harrowing vision for the future of consumer protection in the United States. His proposals to dismantle the Consumer Financial Protection Bureau (CFPB) under the guise of promoting economic efficiency and reducing bureaucracy threaten to leave consumers vulnerable and the financial system precariously exposed to instability and abuse.

Bowes begins by criticizing the CFPB as an overreaching and burdensome agency that imposes excessive costs on businesses, particularly small financial institutions. He argues that the CFPB stifles economic growth through its stringent regulations. However, this perspective dangerously underestimates the critical role the CFPB plays in protecting consumers from predatory practices and financial exploitation. By advocating for the dismantling of the CFPB, Bowes seeks to remove essential protections that prevent abusive practices in the financial sector, leaving consumers defenseless against fraud.

One of the most alarming aspects of Bowes' argument is his call to significantly reduce the CFPB's enforcement powers. He suggests that a lighter regulatory touch would encourage innovation and competition. However, robust enforcement is necessary to deter bad actors and ensure fair practices in the financial market. Weakening the CFPB's enforcement capabilities could lead to an increase in fraudulent activities, as businesses may feel emboldened to cut corners without fear of significant repercussions. This would erode public trust in the financial system and potentially lead to great economic harm.

Moreover, Bowes advocates for shifting the CFPB's responsibilities to other regulatory bodies, arguing that this would streamline regulatory processes. This approach overlooks the specialized focus and expertise that the CFPB brings to consumer protection. Other agencies may lack the specific mandate and resources to effectively oversee consumer financial products and services. Diluting the CFPB's responsibilities would likely result in less rigorous oversight and weaker consumer protections, making financial markets more dangerous for the average consumer.

Bowes also contends that the CFPB's regulatory framework is too complex and costly for financial institutions to navigate. While some regulatory simplification may be warranted, Bowes' broad call for deregulation risks dismantling crucial safeguards. The CFPB's regulations are designed to prevent abusive practices and ensure transparency in financial products. Removing these protections could lead to a resurgence of the very practices that precipitated the 2008 financial crisis, such as predatory lending and deceptive mortgage practices.

Furthermore, Bowes' emphasis on reducing bureaucracy often overlooks the benefits of comprehensive consumer protection. The CFPB has returned billions of dollars to consumers through enforcement actions against financial misconduct. By advocating for its dismantling, Bowes undermines an agency that has been instrumental in securing financial justice for millions of Americans. His proposals would disproportionately harm the most vulnerable consumers, who rely on the CFPB's protections to safeguard their financial well-being. Bowes' approach disregards the broader role of the CFPB in maintaining global financial stability. In an interconnected world, robust financial regulation in one country can have positive ripple effects globally. Weakening the regulatory framework in the U.S. could undermine international efforts to promote financial stability and cooperation, isolating the U.S. from global standards, leading to conflicts in international finance.

In conclusion, "Independent Regulatory Agencies: Consumer Protection Bureau" by Robert Bowes advocates for dismantling the CPB under the guise of promoting efficiency and reducing bureaucracy. The CPB plays an essential role in protecting consumers from predatory practices and ensuring fair treatment in the financial marketplace. Bowes' vision, if implemented, would lead to significant consumer harm and destabilize the economy, making his recommendations deeply offensive to the public good.

144

Why We Can't Trust Robert Bowes

We cannot trust Robert Bowes because his background and actions reveal a consistent pattern of advocating for policies that prioritize deregulation and reduced consumer protections, often ignoring the critical safeguards necessary for a fair and stable financial system. As a senior fellow at the Heritage Foundation, Bowes has been a vocal proponent of dismantling regulatory frameworks that protect consumers from financial abuses and predatory practices.

One significant example of Bowes' controversial stance is his persistent call for dismantling the Consumer Financial Protection Bureau (CFPB). Bowes argues that the CFPB imposes excessive burdens on businesses and stifles economic growth. However, this perspective dangerously downplays the essential role the CFPB plays in safeguarding consumers against predatory practices and financial exploitation. During his tenure at the Heritage Foundation, Bowes has consistently pushed for policies that prioritize short-term business interests over long-term consumer protections, risking the resurgence of abusive practices that led to the 2008 financial crisis.

Moreover, Bowes' advocacy for reducing the CFPB's enforcement powers reflects a troubling disregard for the importance of robust oversight in the financial sector. He suggests that a lighter regulatory touch would encourage innovation and competition. However, weakening the CFPB's enforcement capabilities would embolden bad actors and increase the likelihood of financial misconduct. Bowes' background includes pushing for deregulation across various sectors, often with little regard for the potential consequences of such actions on consumer safety and market stability.

In summary, Robert Bowes' background and actions indicate a clear preference for deregulation and reduced oversight without adequately considering the essential protections these frameworks provide to consumers. His proposals, while aimed at promoting economic efficiency, risk undermining financial stability, enabling corporate malfeasance, and leaving consumers vulnerable to exploitation. Bowes' policies reflect an untrustworthy approach that prioritizes short-term gains over the long-term health and integrity of the financial system, making his recommendations deeply bothering and potentially harmful.

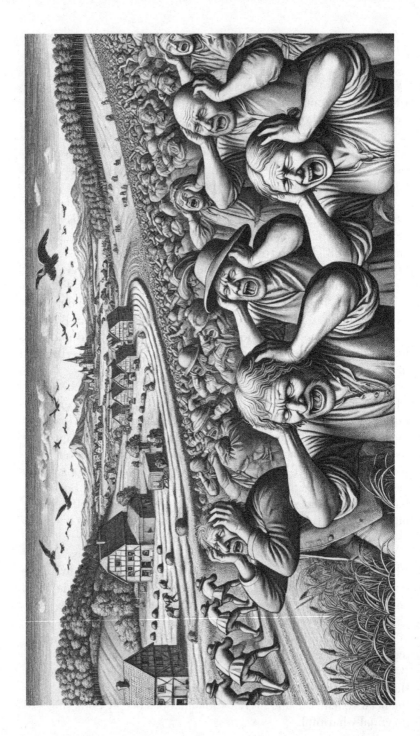

Section 5:
Independent Regulatory Agencies
28 Federal Communications Commission
by Brendan Carr

- A Cautionary Tale

Come closer, everyone, for the tale you are about to hear will fill your heart with dread. "Independent Regulatory Agencies" Federal Communications Commission," by Brendan Carr presents a deeply troubling blueprint for the future of communications regulation. His proposals, aimed at reducing the FCC's oversight and promoting deregulatory policies, pose risks to consumer protections, media diversity, and the integrity of the telecommunications landscape.

Carr begins by arguing that the FCC's regulatory framework stifles innovation and burdens businesses with unnecessary compliance costs. He advocates for a substantial reduction in the agency's regulatory authority, suggesting that less oversight would foster a more competitive and dynamic market. However, this perspective dangerously underestimates the crucial role the FCC plays in maintaining fair competition, protecting consumers, and ensuring a diverse media environment. By advocating for sweeping deregulation, Carr threatens to dismantle essential safeguards that prevent monopolistic practices and access to communication services.

One of the most alarming aspects of Carr's proposals is his push to eliminate net neutrality regulations. Net neutrality is fundamental to ensuring that internet service providers (ISPs) treat all data equally and do not discriminate against or favor certain websites or services. Without these protections, ISPs could prioritize their own content or that of paying partners, stifling competition and limiting consumer choice. Carr's vision would allow ISPs to engage in throttling, blocking, and paid prioritization, leading to a fragmented and unfair internet landscape that undermines an open and free internet.

Moreover, Carr's call to reduce the FCC's oversight extends to the ownership rules that promote media diversity. He argues that relaxing these rules would lead to greater efficiencies and innovation. However, weakening media ownership regulations risks consolidating media power in the hands of a few large corporations, reducing the diversity of viewpoints and local news coverage. This consolidation would undermine the democratic principles of a free and independent press, leaving communities with fewer sources of information and diminishing the public's ability to hold power accountable.

Carr also targets the Lifeline program, which provides subsidized phone and internet services to low-income households. He contends that the program is fraught with fraud and inefficiency and suggests scaling it back significantly. While the program has faced challenges, it plays a vital role in bridging the digital divide and ensuring that vulnerable populations have access to essential communication services. Gutting the Lifeline program would disproportionately harm low-income families, seniors, and rural communities, exacerbating existing inequalities and leaving millions disconnected from critical resources.

Furthermore, Carr's emphasis on reducing regulatory barriers for 5G deployment overlooks the need for balanced policies that also address public health and environmental concerns. Rapid deployment without adequate oversight could lead to infrastructure rollouts that prioritize speed over safety and community impact. Carr's proposals risk sidelining local authorities and communities in decision-making processes, undermining public trust and potentially exposing the public to unforeseen risks.

In addition, Carr's deregulatory agenda threatens the FCC's ability to enforce important consumer protections, such as privacy regulations and rules against deceptive advertising practices. By weakening the FCC's enforcement powers, Carr's plan would leave consumers more vulnerable to exploitation and abuse by unscrupulous actors in the telecommunications industry, eroding confidence in communication services that could lead to widespread consumer distrust and harm.

In conclusion, "Independent Regulatory Agencies: Federal Communications Commission" by Brendan Carr advocates for a drastic reduction in the FCC's regulatory authority under the pretext of promoting innovation and competition. However, his proposals pose significant threats to consumer protections, media diversity, and the integrity of the telecommunications landscape. The FCC plays a critical role in ensuring fair competition, protecting consumers, and maintaining a diverse and democratic media environment.

Why We Can't Trust Brendan Carr

We cannot trust Brendan Carr because his background and actions reveal a consistent pattern of advocating for deregulation and reduced oversight, which often endangers consumer protections and media diversity. As an FCC Commissioner, Carr has been a prominent supporter of policies that prioritize corporate interests over the public good, significantly impacting the fairness and accessibility of communication services.

One significant example of Carr's controversial stance is his strong opposition to net neutrality. During his tenure at the FCC, Carr played a key role in repealing net neutrality regulations, arguing that such rules stifled innovation and investment in broadband infrastructure. However, this perspective dangerously overlooks the critical role net neutrality plays in ensuring an open and fair internet. Without these protections, internet service providers (ISPs) can engage in practices like throttling, blocking, and paid prioritization, which can limit consumer choice and stifle competition. Carr's actions have paved the way for ISPs to potentially exploit their power, undermining the principles of a free and open internet.

Moreover, Carr has consistently pushed for reducing regulatory barriers for 5G deployment without adequately addressing public health and environmental concerns. His background includes advocating for policies that fast-track infrastructure rollouts, sidelining local authorities and minimizing public input. This approach prioritizes industry interests over community welfare, leading to infrastructure decisions that may prioritize speed and cost over safety and community impact. Carr's disregard for these important considerations reflects an untrustworthy approach that compromises public health and safety.

In summary, Brendan Carr's background and actions indicate a preference for deregulation and reduced oversight, which can undermine essential consumer protections and media diversity. His advocacy for repealing net neutrality and fast-tracking 5G deployment without adequate safeguards reflects an approach that prioritizes corporate interests over the public good, making his policies deeply biased, authoritarian, and harmful to the public.

150

Section 5:
Independent Regulatory Agencies
29 Federal Election Commission
by Hans A. von Spakovsky

- A Cautionary Tale

Folks, get ready, because you are about to hear a story for disturbing than you could ever imagine. "Independent Regulatory Agencies: Federal Election Commission," by Hans A. von Spakovsky presents a chilling vision for the future of election oversight. His proposals to overhaul the FEC and reduce its regulatory powers threaten to undermine the integrity of U.S. elections, weaken protections against campaign finance abuses, and erode trust in the democratic process.

Von Spakovsky begins by arguing that the FEC's current structure and regulations are overly burdensome and stifle political participation. He advocates for reducing the commission's enforcement capabilities and scaling back its regulatory framework. However, this perspective dangerously underestimates the critical role the FEC plays in ensuring transparency and fairness in elections. By advocating for sweeping deregulation, Von Spakovsky risks dismantling essential safeguards that prevent corruption and ensure that elections are conducted fairly and openly.

One of the most alarming aspects of Von Spakovsky's proposals is his call to shift the FEC's enforcement responsibilities to other bodies or eliminate them entirely. He suggests that the agency's role should be limited to advisory and educational functions rather than enforcement. This approach would effectively neuter the FEC's ability to hold violators accountable, allowing campaign finance abuses to proliferate unchecked. Without robust enforcement, powerful interests could exert undue influence over elections, undermining the principle of one person, one vote.

Moreover, Von Spakovsky's advocacy for reducing the FEC's regulatory reach extends to campaign finance disclosure requirements. He argues that current disclosure rules are too burdensome and infringe on free speech rights. However, disclosure is fundamental to ensuring that voters can see who is funding political campaigns and influence. By pushing for relaxed disclosure

151

requirements, Von Spakovsky's vision would make it easier for dark money to flow into elections, obscuring the true sources of campaign funding and making it harder for voters to make informed decisions.

Von Spakovsky also proposes changing the FEC's bipartisan structure, arguing that the current setup leads to gridlock and inefficiency. He suggests moving to a single-administrator model or other configurations that would ostensibly streamline decision-making. However, this change could politicize the commission further, allowing a single party or individual to wield disproportionate power over election oversight. The current bipartisan structure, while not perfect, is designed to ensure that both major political parties have a say in how elections are regulated and overseen.

Furthermore, Von Spakovsky's emphasis on reducing regulatory barriers for political activity overlooks the need for balanced policies that ensure fair competition and prevent abuses. Rapid deregulation without adequate safeguards could lead to a political environment where wealthy donors and special interests dominate the electoral process. This would undermine the democratic principles of equity and fairness, leading to greater political inequality and the disenfranchisement of ordinary voters. Von Spakovsky's deregulatory agenda threatens the FEC's ability to enforce crucial campaign finance laws and regulations. By weakening the FEC's enforcement powers, his plan would leave elections more vulnerable to manipulation and corruption by unscrupulous actors. This would erode public confidence in the electoral system and could lead to widespread disillusionment and disengagement among voters.

In conclusion, "Independent Regulatory Agencies: Federal Trade Commission" by Hans A. Von Spakovsky calls for a drastic reduction in the FEC's regulatory authority under the pretext of promoting political participation and efficiency. However, his proposals pose significant threats to the integrity of U.S. elections, transparency in campaign finance, and public trust in the democratic process. The FEC plays a critical role in ensuring fair and transparent elections, protecting against corruption, and maintaining public confidence in the electoral system. Von Spakovsky's vision will lead to increased corruption, reduced transparency, and more inequality in the political process, making his recommendations deeply disquieting and suspect.

Why We Can't Trust Hans A. von Spakovsky

We cannot trust Hans A. Von Spakovsky because his background and actions reveal a consistent pattern of advocating for policies that undermine the integrity of the electoral process and reduce essential safeguards. As a senior fellow at the Heritage Foundation and a former member of the Federal Election Commission (FEC), Von Spakovsky has been a vocal proponent of measures that could weaken the oversight and enforcement capabilities of election regulatory bodies.

One significant example of Von Spakovsky's controversial stance is his persistent call to reduce the FEC's enforcement powers. He argues that the FEC should focus on advisory and educational roles rather than enforcing campaign finance laws. During his tenure at the FEC, Von Spakovsky pushed for less stringent regulations and enforcement, a stance that risks allowing campaign finance abuses to go unchecked. Moreover, Von Spakovsky's advocacy for relaxed campaign finance disclosure requirements raises serious concerns. He contends that current disclosure rules infringe on free speech rights, yet these rules are crucial for transparency, allowing voters to see who is funding political campaigns, ensuring democratic accountability and fairness.

Hans A. Von Spakovsky's background and actions indicate a preference for deregulation and reduced oversight, which can undermine the integrity of the electoral process. His deregulatory agenda threatens the FEC's ability to enforce crucial campaign finance laws and regulations. By weakening the FEC's enforcement powers, his plan would leave elections more vulnerable to manipulation and corruption by unscrupulous actors. This would erode public confidence in the electoral system and could lead to widespread disillusionment and disengagement among voters.

In conclusion, "Independent Regulatory Agencies: Federal Election Commission" by Hans A. Von Spakovsky advocates for a drastic reduction in the FEC's regulatory authority under the pretext of promoting political participation and efficiency. His proposals pose significant threats to the integrity of U.S. elections, transparency in campaign finance, and public trust in the democratic process and will result in more corruption, less transparency, and political inequality.

Section 5:
Independent Regulatory Agencies
30 Federal Trade Commission
by Adam Candeub

- A Cautionary Tale

Gather 'round, friends, the account that is about to be revealed will send chills down your spine. "Independent Regulatory Agencies: Federal Trade Commission," by Adam Candeub presents a terrifying blueprint for the future of consumer protection and competition oversight in the United States. His proposals to drastically reduce the FTC's regulatory authority and enforcement capabilities pose significant risks to consumer welfare, market fairness, and the integrity of the economic system.

Candeub begins by arguing that the FTC's current structure and regulatory framework are overly burdensome and stifle innovation. He advocates for reducing the commission's regulatory scope and scaling back its enforcement powers. However, this perspective dangerously underestimates the critical role the FTC plays in protecting consumers from fraudulent, deceptive, and unfair business practices. By pushing for sweeping deregulation, Candeub risks dismantling essential safeguards that ensure markets operate fairly and that consumers are not exploited.

One of the most alarming aspects of Candeub's proposals is his call to limit the FTC's ability to enforce antitrust laws. He suggests that the agency's focus should be shifted away from aggressive antitrust enforcement to a more lenient approach that emphasizes market freedom. This approach could embolden monopolistic practices and allow large corporations to dominate markets without fear of repercussion. Weakening antitrust enforcement would undermine competition, reduce consumer choice, and lead to higher prices and lower quality products and services.

Moreover, Candeub advocates for reducing the FTC's role in protecting consumer privacy. He argues that stringent privacy regulations hinder business operations and innovation. However, in an era where data breaches and misuse of personal information are rampant, strong privacy protections are more important than ever. By relaxing privacy regulations, Candeub's vision would leave consumers more vulnerable to exploitation and abuse, eroding trust in the digital economy and compromising individuals' control over their personal data.

Candeub also targets the FTC's authority to regulate advertising practices, suggesting that current regulations are overly restrictive and stifle commercial speech. While he frames this as a way to promote free expression, it overlooks the FTC's crucial role in preventing false and misleading advertising. Without robust oversight, deceptive advertising practices could proliferate, misleading consumers and undermining fair competition. Candeub's proposals would weaken the protections that ensure consumers receive accurate information, leading to increased exploitation and economic harm.

Furthermore, Candeub's emphasis on reducing the FTC's regulatory barriers for businesses overlooks the need for balanced policies that protect consumers and ensure market integrity. Rapid deregulation without adequate safeguards could lead to a marketplace where powerful interests dominate, and consumer rights are neglected. This would exacerbate economic inequality and reduce the overall trust in the economic system. Candeub's vision risks creating a regulatory environment where corporate profits are prioritized over consumer welfare and market fairness. Candeub's deregulatory agenda threatens the FTC's ability to enforce critical consumer protection laws and regulations. By weakening the FTC's enforcement powers, his plan would leave consumers more vulnerable to fraud, deception, and unfair practices by unscrupulous businesses. This would erode public confidence in the marketplace and could lead to widespread disillusionment and disengagement among consumers.

In conclusion, "ONWARD!" by Adam Candeub advocates for a drastic reduction in the FTC's regulatory authority under the guise of promoting innovation and market freedom. However, his proposals pose significant threats to consumer protection, market fairness, and the integrity of the economic system. The FTC plays a critical role in ensuring fair competition, protecting consumers, and maintaining trust in the marketplace. Candeub's vision, will lead to increased corporate abuse, reduced protections, and economic inequality, making his recommendations deeply unnerving and untrustworthy.

Why We Can't Trust Adam Candeub

We cannot trust Adam Candeub because his background and actions reveal a consistent pattern of advocating for extreme deregulation and reduced oversight, often at the expense of consumer protections and market fairness. As a law professor and former acting assistant secretary at the U.S. Department of Commerce, Candeub has a history of pushing for policies that prioritize corporate interests over consumer welfare.

One significant example of Candeub's controversial stance is his advocacy for limiting the Federal Trade Commission's (FTC) enforcement powers. During his tenure at the Department of Commerce, Candeub supported deregulatory measures that weakened consumer protections in the digital marketplace. His proposals to reduce the FTC's regulatory scope and shift away from aggressive antitrust enforcement risk allowing monopolistic practices to flourish, which could lead to reduced competition, higher prices, and lower quality products and services for consumers.

Moreover, Candeub's stance on privacy regulations is particularly concerning. He argues that stringent privacy protections hinder business operations and innovation. However, in an era where data breaches and misuse of personal information are rampant, strong privacy regulations are more important than ever. Candeub's background includes advocating for policies that prioritize business interests over consumer privacy, potentially leaving individuals more vulnerable to exploitation and abuse. This disregard for consumer privacy highlights a troubling lack of concern for the well-being and rights of individuals in the digital age.

In summary, Adam Candeub's background and actions indicate a preference for extreme deregulation and reduced oversight, which can undermine essential consumer protections and market fairness. His advocacy for limiting the FTC's enforcement powers and relaxing privacy regulations reflects an untrustworthy approach that prioritizes corporate interests over the public good. Candeub's policies, if implemented, could lead to increased corporate abuse, reduced consumer protections, and greater economic inequality, making his recommendations deeply disturbing and harmful to the public.

ONWARD!
by Edwin Feulner

Attention, everyone, last chance, the story does come to an end, for better or worse. Edwin Feulner's concluding chapter "Onwards" in Project 2025 closes with a vision for America's future that is both alarming and fraught with risks. Feulner, co-founder of the Heritage Foundation, outlines a strategy to reshape the country's political and economic landscape through aggressive deregulation, reduced government oversight, and a return to conservative principles. While Feulner's rhetoric is imbued with optimism about American renewal, his proposals carry significant dangers for social equity, environmental sustainability, and economic stability.

Feulner begins by extolling the virtues of limited government and free-market capitalism. He argues that excessive regulation and government intervention stifle innovation and economic growth. However, this perspective dangerously underestimates the critical role that government oversight plays in protecting public welfare and ensuring fair market practices. Deregulation, as Feulner proposes, often leads to unchecked corporate power, which can result in exploitative practices, environmental degradation, and economic inequality.

One of the most alarming aspects of Feulner's vision is his call for extensive cuts to social welfare programs. He contends that reducing government spending on social services will encourage personal responsibility and self-reliance. However, this approach overlooks the essential support that these programs provide to millions of Americans, including the elderly, disabled, and economically disadvantaged. By dismantling these safety nets, Feulner's proposals risk exacerbating poverty and widening the gap between the wealthy and the poor.

Additionally, Feulner's policies reflect a patriarchal bias that disproportionately affects women and minorities. His support for reducing social welfare programs and deregulating industries results in greater economic hardship for these groups, who are more likely to rely on such support due to systemic inequalities. Women and minorities, who already face significant barrier in the workforce and broader society, would be further marginalized by Feulner's agenda, increasing gender and racial disparities and perpetuating a cycle of disadvantage. Feulner's support for policies that restrict women's reproductive rights highlights a broader agenda that undermines women's bodily autonomy. By backing measures that limit access to healthcare and reproductive services, Feulner's approach disproportionately affects women, exacerbating gender inequality and stripping away critical protections for women's health and rights.

Moreover, Feulner advocates for a significant rollback of environmental regulations. He argues that such regulations impose unnecessary burdens on businesses and hinder economic growth. However, this perspective fails to recognize the critical importance of environmental protections in safeguarding public health and combating climate change. Deregulating environmental standards would likely lead to increased pollution, natural resource depletion, and a hastening of the climate crisis, with devastating long-term consequences for the planet and future generations.

Feulner also pushes for a more robust defense policy, emphasizing increased military spending and a stronger global presence. While national security is undeniably important, Feulner's approach risks escalating international tensions and diverting resources away from essential domestic needs such as education, healthcare, and infrastructure. This militaristic stance could lead to a more aggressive foreign policy, increasing the likelihood of conflict and undermining global stability.

In addition, Feulner's emphasis on reducing taxes for businesses and wealthy individuals is deeply concerning. He argues that lower taxes will spur economic growth and create jobs. However, this trickle-down economic theory has been widely discredited, as it often results in increased wealth concentration at the top while providing minimal benefits to the broader population. Reducing taxes for the wealthy and corporations without ensuring equitable redistribution can exacerbate economic inequality and undermine social cohesion.

Perhaps most alarming is Feulner's championing of Schedule F, a controversial policy aimed at dismantling government bureaucracy. This move threatens to destabilize essential public services by making it easier to fire federal employees undermining effectiveness of the civil service, this lack of stability is an assault on governance and freedom.

Why We Can't Trust Edwin Feulner

We cannot trust Edwin Feulner because his background and actions consistently reveal a pattern of advocating for policies that prioritize corporate interests and conservative ideologies over social equity, environmental sustainability, and economic stability. As co-founder and long-time president of the Heritage Foundation, Feulner has promoted a vision that often disregards the broader public good in favor of deregulation, reduced government oversight, and aggressive tax cuts for the wealthy.

One significant example of Feulner's controversial stance is his unwavering support for extensive deregulation. Throughout his career at the Heritage Foundation, Feulner has pushed for rolling back environmental protections, arguing that they hinder economic growth. However, this perspective dangerously underestimates the importance of these regulations in protecting public health and combating climate change. Feulner's advocacy for deregulation threatens to increase pollution and accelerate environmental degradation, posing severe risks to both current and future generations. His actions demonstrate a troubling disregard for the long-term consequences of environmental neglect in favor of short-term economic gains.

Moreover, Feulner's approach to social welfare programs is deeply troubling. He has consistently argued for significant cuts to social services, suggesting that such measures will foster personal responsibility and reduce government spending. However, this perspective ignores the essential support these programs provide to millions of vulnerable Americans, including the elderly, disabled, and economically disadvantaged. By dismantling these safety nets, Feulner's policies risk exacerbating poverty and widening the gap between the wealthy and the poor, undermining social cohesion and stability. His history of promoting austerity measures during his time at the Heritage Foundation shows a clear preference for policies that benefit the affluent at the expense of those in need.

Additionally, Feulner's policies reflect a patriarchal bias that disproportionately affects women and minorities. His support for reducing social welfare programs and deregulating industries often results in greater economic hardship for these groups, who are more likely to rely on such support due to systemic inequalities. Women and minorities, who already face significant barriers in the workforce and broader society, would be further marginalized by Feulner's agenda, increasing gender and racial disparities and perpetuating a cycle of disadvantage. Feulner's long-standing association with conservative think tanks that oppose gender equality measures further underscores his lack of commitment to advancing women's and minority rights.

Furthermore, Feulner's stance on women's bodily autonomy is deeply troubling. He supports policies that restrict reproductive rights, thereby undermining women's autonomy over their own bodies. By backing measures that limit access to healthcare and reproductive services, Feulner's approach disproportionately affects women, exacerbating gender inequality and stripping away critical protections for women's health and rights. His long-standing opposition to reproductive rights highlights a broader agenda that seeks to control and limit women's freedoms.

Feulner's advocacy for Schedule F, a policy aimed at dismantling government bureaucracy, is another example of his untrustworthy approach. Schedule F would make it easier to fire federal employees, undermining the stability and effectiveness of the civil service. This move threatens to destabilize essential public services by allowing for political purges and reducing the independence of federal agencies. Feulner's support for this policy reflects his broader agenda of reducing government oversight and weakening the institutions designed to protect public interests.

In summary, Edwin Feulner's background and actions reveal a clear preference for policies that prioritize far right ideologies and corporate interests over the well-being of the broader population. His support for extensive deregulation, cuts to social welfare programs, Schedule F, and restrictive reproductive policies reflects an untrustworthy approach that fails to consider the critical protections necessary for a fair and just society. Feulner's policies, if implemented, could lead to greater economic inequality, environmental harm, and social instability, making his recommendations insultingly outrageous and undoubtably harmful.

Additional Project 2025 Contributors

Alabama Policy Institute
Alliance Defending Freedom
America First Legal
American Accountability Foundation
American Association of Pro-Life Obstetricians and Gynecologists
ACLJ Action
American Compass
American Cornerstone Institute
American Council of Trustees and Alumni
American Family Association
American Family Project
American Legislative Exchange Council
American Juris Link
AMAC Action
American Moment
American Principles Project
California Family Council
Center for Equal Opportunity
Center for Family and Human Rights
Center for Immigration Studies
Center for Renewing America
Claremont Institute
Coalition for a Prosperous America
Competitive Enterprise Institute
Concerned Women for America
Conservative Partnership Institute
Defense of Freedom Institute
Ethics and Public Policy Center
Family Policy Alliance
Family Research Council
Feds for Medical Freedom
First Liberty Institute
Forge Leadership Network
Foundation for American Innovation
Foundation for Defense of Democracies
Foundation for Government Accountability
Frederick Douglass Foundation
FreedomWorks
Heartland Institute
Heritage Foundation
Hillsdale College
Honest Elections Project
Independent Women's Forum

Institute for Education Reform
Institute for Energy Research
Institute for the American Worker
Institute for Women's Health
Intercollegiate Studies Institute
James Madison Institute
Job Creators Network
Keystone Policy
Liberty University
Media Research Center
Mississippi Center for Public Policy
Moms for Liberty
National Association of Scholars
National Center for Public Policy Research
Noah Webster Educational Foundation
Oklahoma Council of Public Affairs
Pacific Research Institute
Patrick Henry College
Personnel Policy Operations
Project 21 Black Leadership Network
Public Interest Legal Foundation
Recovery for America Now Foundation
Susan B. Anthony Pro-Life America
Tea Party Patriots
Teneo Network
Texas Public Policy Foundation
The American Conservative
The American Main Street Initiative
The Leadership Institute
Turning Point USA
Young America's Foundation
1792 Exchange

These organizations, with their far right patriarchal, racist, and religious views, use economic agendas to overshadow their regressive goals of overturning a century of progress for women and minorities. By aggressively pushing for deregulation, tax cuts for the wealthy, and reduced government oversight, they mask their underlying intention to dismantle protections and rights that have been hard-won over decades. Their economic policies promise growth and prosperity, but in reality, they often lead to increased inequality, disproportionately affecting women and minorities who rely on social services and regulatory protections to ensure fair treatment and opportunities in the workplace and society. These are organizations to distrust.

Individual Millionaire and Billionaire Backers

Project 2025 is significantly backed by some of the wealthiest individuals and families in the United States, many of whom are known for their extensive influence in conservative politics. These are traitors to America and what she stands for. Here are 25 of the top millionaire and billionaire backers, listed in order of contribution:

Leonard Leo - Known for his extensive work in reshaping the judiciary, Leo has funneled millions through dark money networks in support.

Charles Koch - The Koch network has directed over $4.4 million to Project 2025, emphasizing deregulation and conservative energy policies.

Harlan Crow - A Texas real estate magnate, Crow has been a significant donor to conservative causes and Project 2025.

Paul Singer - A hedge fund billionaire, Singer has heavily financed conservative initiatives, including those under Project 2025.

Robert Mercer - The hedge fund manager and prominent Trump supporter has contributed substantially to the project.

Rebekah Mercer - Robert Mercer's daughter, also a major conservative donor, heavily involved in funding Project 2025.

Ken Griffin - The billionaire hedge fund manager has been a notable contributor to various conservative causes.

Sheldon Adelson - Before his death, Adelson was a major GOP donor, with his estate continuing to support conservative agendas.

Richard Uihlein - The Uline CEO has been a prolific donor to right-wing causes and candidates.

Betsy DeVos - The former Education Secretary and her family are long-time supporters of conservative education reform and Project 2025.

Peter Thiel - The tech billionaire and Trump supporter has funded numerous conservative projects, including Project 2025.

Joe Ricketts - Founder of TD Ameritrade, Ricketts has been a significant funder of conservative initiatives.

Timothy Mellon - Heir to the Mellon fortune, he has donated millions to conservative causes.

Bernard Marcus - Co-founder of Home Depot, Marcus has been a major financial backer of conservative policies.

Foster Friess - The late investor and philanthropist was known for his generous donations to conservative causes.

Phil Anschutz - A billionaire with deep investments in conservative media and political movements.

Isaac Perlmutter - Former Marvel CEO, Perlmutter has been a significant donor to conservative campaigns.

Bruce Kovner - A hedge fund billionaire who has supported numerous conservative think tanks and initiatives.

Dick DeVos - Betsy DeVos' husband, also a significant funder of conservative education reform.

Thomas Wachtell - An investor known for his substantial contributions to conservative political causes.

Ron Cameron - Agribusiness tycoon, Cameron has been a major donor to right-wing political movements.

Sanford Diller - The late real estate mogul was a prominent supporter of conservative causes.

George Roberts - Co-founder of global investment company KKR, Roberts has contributed extensively to conservative political campaigns.

Jeffrey Yass - A financier who has donated millions to conservative political action committees.

Randy Kendrick - The wife of Arizona Diamondbacks owner Ken Kendrick, she has been a major donor to conservative causes.

Note on Greed

The sheer greed and hypocrisy of these organizations, backed by their billionaire patrons, and individual backers, is staggering. They loudly champion free-market principles and reduced government intervention, yet they are the first to benefit from corporate welfare and tax breaks that disproportionately favor the wealthy. This blatant hypocrisy undermines their claims of advocating for fairness and opportunity. Their billionaire backers pour vast sums into these organizations to ensure that policies tilt ever more in their favor, exacerbating economic inequality and entrenching their power. They masquerade their self-serving agendas as noble efforts to spur economic growth while quietly reaping enormous financial rewards at the expense of the most vulnerable. These are unpatriotic folks. They are not "Christian" in any recognizable sense of Jesus or his teachings.

The dishonor and corruption within these organizations is deeply entrenched. They wield their financial power to influence legislation and regulatory decisions, ensuring that their interests are protected and advanced. This manipulation of the political system often results in policies that strip away protections for workers, consumers, and the environment, while offering little more than lip service to issues of social justice. Their actions speak louder than their rhetoric, revealing a profound disregard for the societal impacts of their greed. They exploit economic agendas to divert attention from their true objectives: consolidating wealth and power, and rolling back decades of progress in civil rights, environmental protections, and social equity. This relentless pursuit of self-interest at the cost of the public good is nothing short of a betrayal of democratic principles and a gross abuse of the power they have accumulated. They are disgusting.

The greed of the wealthy backers behind Project 2025, cloaked in the rhetoric of freedom and economic efficiency, reveals a terrifying agenda that threatens to enslave society to their interests. A society cannot be half free and half slave; as long as these powerful interests dominate, the majority remain shackled by economic disparity and social inequity. True freedom demands that all individuals have equal opportunity and protection under the law, free from the abusive manipulations of those who would exploit them for personal gain. Only by rejecting this false freedom and standing against the greed of these powerful elites can we ensure a just and equitable society for all.

In Conclusion

As we stand on the precipice of an uncertain future, it is imperative to examine the chilling implications of Project 2025. This ambitious endeavor, championed by the Heritage Foundation and its allies, aims to reshape the American political landscape in ways that could have devastating consequences for our democracy, our economy, and our very way of life. Project 2025 is not merely a collection of policy proposals; it is a blueprint for a Christo-fascist ideology that seeks to impose a theocratic vision on our secular republic, while simultaneously advancing the interests of unbridled capitalism and promoting a relentless agenda of deregulation.

At its core, Project 2025 is driven by a Christo-fascist ideology that seeks to merge religious dogma with state power. This vision is deeply rooted in the belief that America is a Christian nation and that its laws and policies should reflect a specific interpretation of "Christian" values. This perspective is profoundly anti-democratic, as it seeks to impose a singular religious viewpoint on a pluralistic society. It threatens the separation of church and state, a foundational principle of our democracy, and undermines the religious freedom of all Americans, particularly those who adhere to different faiths or none at all.

The proponents of Project 2025 argue that their vision is about restoring moral order and defending traditional values. However, this rhetoric masks a more insidious agenda. The Christo-fascist ideology embedded in Project 2025 seeks to roll back hard-won rights and freedoms, particularly for women, LGBTQ+ individuals, and religious minorities. It envisions a society where religious conformity is enforced through the power of the state, where dissent is suppressed, and theocratic leaders dictate the terms of public and private life.

This ideology is not only about imposing a particular set of religious beliefs but also about consolidating power in the hands of a select few. It is deeply intertwined with a broader agenda of capitalism and deregulation, which seeks to dismantle the regulatory state and unleash the full force of market fundamentalism. The economic vision of Project 2025 is one of unfettered capitalism, where the interests of corporations and the wealthy are prioritized over the needs of ordinary Americans.

The deregulatory agenda of Project 2025 aims to roll back critical protections for workers, consumers, and the environment. This vision is rooted in the belief that government intervention is inherently harmful and that the free market should be the primary arbiter of economic and social outcomes. However, this perspective ignores the profound inequalities and injustices that arise in an unregulated market. It fails to acknowledge the essential role that government plays in safeguarding public health, protecting the environment, and ensuring fair labor practices.

Under the guise of promoting economic freedom, Project 2025 seeks to dismantle the regulatory frameworks that have been established to protect the public from corporate abuses. It envisions a world where environmental regulations are gutted, allowing polluters to ravage our natural resources and poison our communities without consequence. It aims to weaken labor protections, making it easier for employers to exploit workers and undermine their rights to fair wages, safe working conditions, and collective bargaining. It seeks to roll back consumer protections, leaving individuals vulnerable to predatory practices and corporate malfeasance.

The economic policies of Project 2025 are not about creating a level playing field or promoting genuine prosperity for all. Instead, they are designed to entrench the power and wealth of a privileged few at the expense of the many. This vision of capitalism is one that is devoid of compassion, equity, and justice. It prioritizes profit over people and seeks to create a society where the wealthy and powerful can operate with impunity, free from the constraints of regulation and accountability.

The confluence of Christo-fascist ideology and unbridled capitalism in Project 2025 represents a profound threat to the principles of democracy, justice, and equality. This project seeks to reshape our institutions and policies in ways that will erode the rights and freedoms of ordinary Americans and entrench the power of a privileged elite. It is a vision that is profoundly anti-democratic, as it seeks to concentrate power in the hands of a few and impose a singular religious and economic orthodoxy on a diverse and pluralistic society.

170

In conclusion, Project 2025 is a dangerous and far-reaching agenda that threatens to undermine the very foundations of our democracy. It seeks to impose a Christo-fascist ideology that is at odds with the principles of religious freedom and pluralism. It promotes an economic vision of unfettered capitalism that prioritizes the interests of the wealthy and powerful over the needs of ordinary Americans. And it advances a deregulatory agenda that threatens to roll back critical protections for workers, consumers, and the environment.

As we look to the future, it is essential that we remain vigilant in defending the principles of democracy, justice, and equality. We must resist the efforts of those who seek to impose a theocratic vision on our secular republic and who seek to dismantle the regulatory frameworks that protect our rights and well-being. The stakes are too high to remain silent or complacent. We must stand up for the values that define us as a nation and work together to build a future that is inclusive, equitable, and just for all.

By framing their agenda as a quest for economic efficiency and freedom, they divert attention from the social ramifications of their policies. For instance, while advocating for lower taxes and reduced welfare programs, they simultaneously support restrictions on reproductive rights and rollbacks of affirmative action, directly attacking the autonomy and advancement of women and minorities. This strategy of using economic arguments as a smokescreen allows them to pursue a conservative social agenda that threatens to erode the significant gains made in gender and racial equality over the past century.

The road ahead will not be easy, and the forces arrayed against us are formidable. But we have faced challenges before, and we have always risen to meet them. By standing together and speaking out against the dangers of Project 2025, we can ensure that our democracy remains strong, our rights are protected, and our future is one of hope and opportunity for all. Let us remain steadfast in our commitment to these principles and work tirelessly to create a better, more just world for generations to come.

List of Prints

About the author

The author lives removed.

Please feel free to burn part or all of this book, safely, as an effigy.

Made in the USA
Monee, IL
24 January 2025

10889818R00104